SUSTO, A FOLK ILLNESS

COMPARATIVE STUDIES OF
HEALTH SYSTEMS AND MEDICAL CARE

Series titles available in paperback

John M. Janzen, *The Quest for Therapy in Lower Zaire*

Margaret M. Lock, *East Asian Medicine in Urban Japan: Varieties of Medical Experience*

Jeanie Schmit Kayser-Jones, *Old, Alone, and Neglected: Care of the Aged in the United States and Scotland*

Arthur Kleinman, *Patients and Healers in the Context of Culture: An Exploration of the Borderland between Anthropology, Medicine, and Psychiatry*

Stephen J. Kunitz, *Disease Change and the Role of Medicine: The Navajo Experience*

Carol Laderman, *Wives and Midwives: Childbirth and Nutrition in Rural Malaysia*

Arthur J. Rubel, Carl W. O'Nell, and Rolando Collado-Ardón, *Susto, a Folk Illness*

SUSTO,
A FOLK ILLNESS

Arthur J. Rubel
Carl W. O'Nell
Rolando Collado-Ardón

With the assistance of
John Krejci and Jean Krejci

University of California Press
Berkeley • *Los Angeles* • *Oxford*

University of California Press
Berkeley and Los Angeles, California

University of California Press, Ltd.
Oxford, England

Library of Congress Cataloging in Publication Data

Rubel, Arthur, J.
Susto, a folk illness.

(Comparative studies of health systems and medical care)
Bibliography: p. 169
Includes index.
1. Zapotec Indians—Diseases.   2. Chinantec Indians—
Diseases.   3. Zapotec Indians—Medicine.   4. Chinantec
Indians—Medicine.   5. Indians of Mexico—Oaxaca (State)—
Diseases.   6. Indians of Mexico—Oaxaca (State)—
Medicines.   7. Folk medicine—Mexico—Oaxaca (State)
I. O'Nell, Carl W., 1925-   .   II. Collado-Ardón, Rolando.
III. Title.   IV. Series. [DNLM: 1. Stress, Psychological—
Complications.   2. Disease—Etiology.   3. Psychophysio-
logic disorders.   4. Medicine, Traditional.   5. Ethno-
psychology. WM 172 R894s]
F1219.3D5R83   1985   616.85'22   84-214
ISBN 0-520-07634-6

Printed in the United States of America

1 2 3 4 5 6 7 8 9

The paper used in this publication meets the minimum requirements of
American National Standard for Information Sciences—Permanence of
Paper for Printed Library Materials, ANSI Z39.48–1984.   ∞

Contents

Acknowledgments

THIS investigation owes much to many. So many that it is truly difficult to know with whom to begin. The late Dr. Ralph Clayton Patrick, formerly a member of the Department of Epidemiology, University of North Carolina, was the teacher whose ideas lie behind many of the conceptualizations we present. He showed why the distribution of health conditions within specific populations is of critical interest to the social anthropologist, and sagaciously helped us to improve early formulations of the research design.

The National Institute of Mental Health supported our search for "Stress Factors in the Etiology of the Susto Syndrome" (RO 1MH16861). Additional funds were provided by the Seminario Medicina del Hombre en su Totalidad of the Secretaria de Salubridad y Asistencia de Méxicó, directed by Dr. Fernando Martínez Cortés. Dr. Martínez Cortés and his colleagues constantly demonstrated their intellectual and practical interest in this research and we are indebted to them for it. The O'Brien Fund of the University of Notre Dame kindly afforded Carl O'Nell the opportunity to begin testing of the "Social Stress Gauge" in Oaxaca in anticipation of data collection, and the Instituto de Investigaciones Antropológicas of Mexico's National Autonomous University provided Arthur Rubel a welcome research appointment during which much of the manuscript was prepared for publication. We are grateful to all of those organizations for their support and interest.

Arthur Rubel wishes to acknowledge with gratitude the continuous support and encouragement of Dr. Bernard Gallin, Chairman, Department of Anthropology at Michigan State University, and Rolando Collado is grateful to Dr. Eleuterio Gonzalez Carbajal and other colleagues of the Departamento de Medicina Social, Preventiva, y Salud Pública of the Universidad Nacional Autónoma de México for their intellectual stimulation and inspiration throughout this investigation.

The ideas which we offer here result from interaction between ourselves and many others. This is especially true of the responses of Dr. Carole Browner and Dr. Nancy O'Nell who have read and reread many of our preliminary efforts to set ideas to paper. They have helped us enormously with their thoughtful criticism. Dr. Alfredo Heredia Duarte, Dr. Scott Swisher, and Dr. Raymond Murray provided able and remarkably constructive criticisms of the clinical findings; we thank them for their willingness to do so despite their already overladen schedules. Professor Philip Dennis helped us improve an early draft with his helpful suggestions. Professor Charles Leslie painstakingly read and criticized a preliminary manuscript. His editorial skills and knowledge of the field have served all of us beyond measure.

The assistance of Dr. Salomon Gallegos in the analysis of the clinical data went well beyond the call of duty and is gratefully acknowledged.

In Oaxaca, we are indebted to Dr. Oscar Martinez, who collected all the samples for examination by the clinical laboratory, and performed most of the physical examinations under trying circumstances. We could not have succeeded without his help. Dr. Fernando Galindo and Dr. Miguel Angel Reyes supervised all the clinical laboratory examinations and counseled us in the techniques to use to collect and preserve blood and stool samples under adverse conditions. They and their laboratory staff consistently accommodated the exigencies of our field work with good humor. The support of these clinicians and of the Oficina de Estudios de Humanidad del Valle de Oaxaca, directed by Mr. Cecil Welte, were simply invaluable. The help of Judi Lynn Anderson made possible the presentation of Chinantec terminology and is gratefully acknowledged.

The panel of scoring physicians was composed of Drs. Noe Castillo and Roberto A. Reyes D. Statistical support was provided by the Computer Center and the Social Science Research and Training Laboratory, University of Notre Dame, and the Unidad de Bioestadística of the Departamento de Medicina Social, Preventiva y Salud Pública of the Universidad Nacional Autónoma de México. Particularly helpful in the statistical treatment of data were Dr. Vasilikie Demos, Dr. Bobby Farrow, Theresa O'Nell Quintero, and Marlyn T. Ritchie. In Mexico, statistical analyses were accomplished with the aid of Dr. Jesus Reynaga Obregón, Dr. Elizabeth Reynoso Ramírez, and Estadístico Jaime García Romero.

Professor Timothy Ready was meticulous in scoring results of the 22-Item Screening Score for Psychiatric Impairment. Keith Bletzer helped with Spanish to English translation of the clinical sections, and H. Sue Henry assisted in the preparation of bibliographic references. Their collaboration was essential to our efforts and is gratefully acknowledged.

We are most appreciative of Martha Reyes, Ursula Traub Greenberg, and Myrna Shoemaker who, in their separate countries, carefully and patiently typed innumerable drafts, which ultimately joined to form this report. Linda Salemka typed the manuscript in its final form and remained patient and constructive in the face of last-minute revisions. We thank them all.

To Vincente Martínez Gutierrez and Señora Rafaela Aragón we are indebted for their informed introduction to Valley Zapotec life, and to ways of combating health problems. Among the Chinantecs, Miguel Hernández Hernández served as interpreter and was invaluable in countless ways. Catarino Lopez shared his medical wisdom, Felipe Hernández Hernández offered endless help as Presidente Municipal and very good friend, and Señora Virginia Martínez Hernández was unfailingly informative and hospitable during the course of our introduction to Chinantec life.

Finally, to all the people whose lives and problems are reflected on these pages, this book is dedicated. For all of us, the opportunity to know well the individuals of these societies and the problems they face remains the most stirring of the many things we will remember from this shared experience.

1

Introduction to Susto

EFFORTS to discover the meaning of illness are a tradition in anthropology. In these pages we seek the meaning of a folk illness known as *susto*. The study was conducted among three different Mexican populations—Mestizo, Zapotec, and Chinantec—in the state of Oaxaca. The following account describes how one young woman became sick with susto when she traveled with her father.

> As they forded the river below their ranch, the swift current swept the father off his feet. He saved himself only by seizing an overhanging vine. The daughter, standing on the bank, watched in alarm. The father reports of his daughter's reaction, as follows: "In fifteen days she was very sick with susto, but I didn't suffer anything. It . . . is very interesting: Some people become ill with susto and others do not even when they suffer the same experience."

As another informant put it:

> It's this way . . . the water contains a being which is its *virtud*, its force or strength, the same as the earth, the woods, the high mountains, and everything. We say that that force steals the strength of humans. It steals our strength and weakens it. To keep this from happening, one must speak to the earth [or water], one must take this action . . . so that our spirit does not remain there.

We hope both to provide new, more relativistic understandings of what it means "to be ill" in other cultures, and to acquire

1

some insight about ourselves. There surely remain few redoubts of ethnocentrism as formidable as explanations of disease causation and the management of illness.*

All societies have been obliged to develop procedures to prevent and treat illnesses. These procedures constitute significant dimensions of a culture and are sensitive to social values: ". . . it is the prevailing philosophic concepts of man which influence his medicine most profoundly" (Pelligrino 1963:10).

We initiated our multidisciplinary investigation of susto (the word itself means fright) with the assumption that we could not understand illness across cultures on the basis of premises produced by our own (Kleinman 1980:378). Consequently, we defined illness as "syndromes from which members of a particular group claim to suffer and for which their culture provides an etiology, a diagnosis, preventive measures, and regimens of healing" (Rubel 1964:268). We sought to build on earlier studies (particularly the works of Bahr et al. 1974; Fabrega and Silver 1973; Frake 1961; Kleinman 1973; G. Lewis 1975; Metzger and Williams 1963) in which the researchers had recorded and scrutinized the manner in which different peoples think about illness. We felt we could not hope to comprehend health and illness anywhere until freed of our own ethnocentrism.

One of the most important goals of anthropological research has been to demonstrate how health understandings and practices elucidate the dominant values, beliefs, and normative expectations of a society and serve as a mirror of the affective qualities of social relationships. Early anthropologists described health institutions much as they discussed the cultural patterns revealed by observations of the family, government, and religion. This tradition persists, for example, in a recent analysis of the rural Costa Rican condition known as *nervios*. Barlett and Low sort

---

* Disease, illness, and sickness will have different referents. *Disease* will henceforth refer to pathological processes, *illness* to the victim's perception and description of discomfort, and *sickness* to acknowledgment of his problem and the response to it by the social group.

out the manifestations of this problem to establish a relationship between the complaint and other dimensions of the lives of these people. They conclude that "the examples of nervios sufferers seem not only to illuminate a complex culture-specific complaint, but also to reveal the most fundamental expectations of life in rural Costa Rica" (1980:554). Morsy (1978) uses another culture-bound syndrome—*uzr*—to elucidate the patterns of social power relationships among Egyptian villagers and goes on to show how her results permit us to better understand the bonds between relatively powerless villages and the central government.

These and other studies have helped demonstrate the functional interrelationship that obtains between health concerns and other value or belief constructs—for example, the relationship between the visitation of illness in a family and a member's having transgressed social norms (Rubel 1966; Vogt 1969:371–374). Marwick's (1965) interpretation of a case of illness as precipitating the fission of subgroups from a parent kinship unit when their social relationships have become insupportable is another case in point. However, Comaroff (1978) has cautioned that the tightness of the researchers' integration of a society's understandings about health with other concepts of its social order represents the analytic efforts of the former more than the thinking of the latter.

In other accounts, researchers have suggested that therapeutic rituals exploit the opportunity presented by a patient's difficulties to resolve interpersonal and intergroup problems and restore social unity (Turner 1967:361–362). In a somewhat different vein, Levi-Strauss considered the trial of a Zuni youth accused of causing a friend's illness as providing the group an opportunity to reaffirm its confidence in the cultural system at large (1963:172–175).

Some studies of folk illnesses have simply assumed that they are psychiatric in nature, ignoring the contribution of organic problems to these complaints even when organic signs and symptoms were observable (Kiev 1968). This "psychologizing" of folk illness has exacerbated the difficulties of separating disease processes from the cultural response to them. Because the presentation of emotional difficulties is even more stylized than presentation of an organic problem, the task of developing cross-cultural evidence about psychological disease conditions has been made the more difficult (Fabrega 1974:40; G. Lewis 1975:93–94; Kleinman 1973:209).

Studies that emphasize traditional healing rituals generally fail to report whether or not the patient recovered or even whether symptoms were alleviated. They sometimes imply that the ritual was efficacious, but present no supporting evidence. For example, Klein, discussing treatments for susto, assures the reader that they are efficacious: ". . . recognizing the cultural and psychological bases for susto cures should not belittle the *physiological effectiveness* of the methods employed; all three dimensions interact in healing to combat the symptoms, which are alleviated in most cases" (Klein 1976:26, emphasis added). Although this claim is plausible, no data to support it are presented. Similar unsupported claims abound in the literature. This romantic idealization of traditional healing, which reverses the more common ethnocentric view, only adds to the difficulty of assessing any kind of healing in unfamiliar cultural settings (Donabedian 1966). Kleinman and Sung reported, in 1979, some of the factors that complicate such an effort. They undertook assessments of patients' symptoms two months after initial treatment at a shrine in Taiwan. Although the patients generally reported themselves to be either cured or significantly improved, the investigators failed to "find conclusive evidence to show that a single case of biological-based disease was effectively treated by the *tang-ki*'s therapy alone." Kleinman and Sung suggest that, prior to an assessment of healing, it is prudent to comprehend all the dimensions of the problems of which patients complain. We are not denying the efficacy of noncosmopolitan systems of healing, but we are recommending that traditional practices be approached with more rigor than has been common (see Finkler 1980).

The extent to which disease is molded by culture remains one of the more provocative issues in anthropology. For instance, the chronic disease commonly known as arthritis or rheumatism and technically recognized as degenerative joint disease appears mainly among older individuals or as a sequel to injuries of a joint. It is found among cultural groups in diverse environments (Lawrence 1966:755–756). Radiological assessments portray degenerating joints, and patients indicate pain on movement or pressure applied to a joint, and complain of weakness. Swelling and enlargements, deformity, atrophy, and shortening of the muscles and abnormalities in the affected skin are easily noted by the trained eye (Edwards 1966:747). With such objective evidence, it is not unreasonable to expect victims to express their discomfort similarly. However, reports of this illness vary systematically among culturally different populations, and even Americans of similar ethnic background have learned to respond differently to it when they are members of different social classes. (Elder and Acheson 1970; Koos 1954). Other reports have shown that Americans complaining of ear, nose, and throat problems systematically emphasize different symptoms depending on their ethnic backgrounds (Zola 1966). Furthermore, even patients' complaints of pain vary according to ethnic group membership (Zborowski 1952). It is clear from this evidence that the objective signs of a given disease process may be molded by the culture and experience of the victim. The distinction between the invariant objective indications of a sickness—the disease—and the way in which the patient describes the problem—the illness— (Eisenberg 1977) is especially important when the complaint is unfamiliar to the researcher. Efforts to "domesticate" exotic health conditions to make them more understandable are described as using the concepts of biomedicine as if they formed a Procrustean bed, contributing to "the degradation of a productive scientific model into a dogma" (Engel 1979:257). The extent to which culture provides the form in which disease becomes illness and then sickness is one of the more fascinating inquiries in cross-cultural research. In a discussion of culture-bound syndromes, Kennedy comments that "most modern scholars tend toward the opinion that these exotic maladies are not clinically distinct syndromes, but are simply the old familiar psychiatric syndromes of the West called by different names and shaped by different cultures" (1973:1152). We disagree with these scholars; our investigation of susto demonstrates how cultural and disease processes interact to form an entity unfamiliar to cosmopolitan medicine.

The cross-cultural study of susto is best approached by fixing attention on the ways in which the patient and his or her family describe the condition: The victim is (1) restless during sleep and (2) otherwise listless, debilitated, depressed, and indifferent to food and to dress and personal hygiene (Sal y Rosas 1958; Gillin 1945; Rubel 1964; Logan 1979; cf. Tousignant 1979:153).

A striking discovery is that this condition is not culture-bound. That is, it is not restricted to a population speaking a distinctive language, or to a singular cultural background. It is found in many cultural groups in North and South America. It is reported among Mexican Americans in the United States (Clark 1959:155–158; Mull and Mull 1981; Martinez and Martin 1966; Rubel 1960; Saunders 1954), in Peru (Gillin 1947; Sal y Rosas 1958; Chiappe Costa 1979; Bolton 1981), in Argentina (Palma 1973; Palma and Torres Vildoza 1974:164, 171), in Colombia (León 1963; Seijas 1972), among Guatemalan groups (Gillin 1945; Adams and Rubel 1967; Logan 1979), and throughout Mexico (Adams and Rubel 1967; O'Nell and Selby 1968; Vogt 1969:370). Moreover, similarly characterized conditions associated with fright are reported in the literature from the Philippines, India, The People's Republic of China, and Taiwan (Hart 1969).

Focusing on the names given to the condition, which is also known locally as *pasmo, tierra, espanto,* and *pérdida de la sombra,* makes it easy to be distracted from the commonalities that exist (Seijas 1972, 1973; O'Nell 1970; Rubel 1970) and, indeed, may sometimes temporarily obscure real differences. In research among the Sibundoy of Colombia, Seijas (1972:177) was eventually obliged to conclude that what they called susto was not the condition described in these pages, but an assortment of pediatric conditions and a catch-all category of adult illnesses for which more usual explanations were socially inappropriate. We use the term *susto* here only when it refers to a cohering set of characteristics that recurs across groups. We fix our attention on a phenomenon, a reality, reported by groups that differ in language and culture. Doing so makes possible comparisons and replication of results.

Rejecting any correlation between what our informants referred to as susto and diseases or functional disorders described in textbooks of cosmopolitan medicine, we began with the assumption that any equivalence that might be established should be based on empirical descriptions of the folk condition. On this matter Comaroff (1978:249) has been helpful:

> Anthropologists have been critical of the indiscriminate application of the bio-medical paradigm to the study of actual medical systems, for it presupposes pre-emptive definitions of relevance. The perspective of scientific medicine is expressed by means of conceptual categories which may well be inappropriate in other medical systems; as a base-line for comparison, it might obscure their particular relevance.

In the Costa Rican research mentioned earlier, Barlett and Low (1980), apparently sharing this viewpoint, prudently refrain from premature biomedical identification of nervios. Complaints of nervios, they report, are regularly attended to by physicians even though they show no equivalence to the kinds of conditions physicians are trained to cure. These researchers record a wide array of symptoms affecting people of both sexes and all ages, with much higher prevalence among two groups—those 19 years of age and older, and women. With such a valuable baseline description in hand, this problem becomes amenable to more finely honed inquiries.

Simons's (1980) work on *latah,* which afflicts large numbers of people in Malaysia and Indonesia and has close counterparts in the Philippines, Taiwan, Thailand, and Burma, is similarly free of a priori assumptions about equivalents in cosmopolitan medicine. Simons finds that most victims of latah are women, tend to be in mid-life when the experience occurs for the first time, and are of relatively low social status. The person suffering from latah typically responds to a startling stimulus with an exaggerated start, often throwing or dropping an object and uttering words ordinarily inappropriate in conversation. Both those studies indicate the fruitfulness of a careful search for explanations in the interaction among biological, emotional, and cultural factors rather than a focus on the pathologies described in textbooks of medicine.

Following some of O'Nell's arguments (1975), Bolton begins his study of susto, or tierra, among the Qolla of Peru with the assumption that it is equivalent to the controversial (Blonde and Riddick 1976; Hale et al. 1975; Permutt et al. 1976) disease that we speak of as hypoglycemia. The study then tries to demonstrate that equivalence by searching for a correlation between having been found severely hypoglycemic at any time in one's life and having ever complained of susto, or tierra. Because hostility is an often reported symptom of hypoglycemia, and the display of such feelings is unacceptable among the Qolla, Bolton concludes that the conditions, although not present at the same time, are one and the same. We will shortly address this issue of whether, in Oaxaca, hypoglycemia is "a perfectly adequate biomedical syndrome" (Bolton 1981:261–262) by which to explain susto.

Suffering susto, being *asustado,* is based on people's understanding that an individual is composed of a body and an immaterial substance, an essence, that may become detached from the body and either wander freely or become a captive of supernatural forces. This essence may leave the body during sleep, particularly when the individual is dreaming, but may also become detached as a consequence of an unsettling or frightening experience. Among Indians, this essence is believed held captive because the patient, wittingly or not, has disturbed the spirit guardians of the earth, river, ponds, forests, or collectivities of animals, birds, or fish. Its release depends upon expiation of the affront. This process dramatically illuminates the relationship that binds humans and suprahumans in these societies.

A social bond of this kind has been described by Bahr and colleagues (1974) in a study of the Pima of northern Mexico. Here again, illness is attributed to the patient's having failed to show deference to the spirit being of a species of animal, fish, or bird, or to the guardian of a locale. The sanction of illness follows transgression of the contractual relationship that binds that species and Pima society, a social contract referred to as the "way." "When way is cited as a causal agent we understand that it is not the individual object which is causing illness but the class of dangerous objects collectively" (p. 65). Further, "the concept of way approximates the concept of a guardian of the species. In this capacity way is implicitly endowed with magical powers. Way is offended the moment an improper action is committed, but the offense is not realized until years later" (p. 73). The southern Mexican groups on which we focus here differ from the Pima in attributing many cases of susto to the startling or frightening effects of an encounter with another human being. Furthermore, by no means all manifestations of such an encounter are delayed; many victims of susto report symptoms within hours or days of an untoward experience.

Some researchers have seen susto as simply a way of explaining mental illness for people who lack the education to understand its true significance. Pages Larraya (1967:18, 23, 71) has identified it as schizophrenia, and León (1963:211; cf. Billig et al. 1948) provides a more sweeping identification:

> Leaving aside infection, poisoning, parasites, nutritional or metabolic processes which can produce problems compatible with the clinical picture and which are capable of producing the condition in its most intractable and dramatic form, the great majority of cases are psychiatric disorders of functional derivation. The circumstances in which the condition makes its appearance and its clinical manifestations indicate the possible presence of at least five entities: a

massive stress reaction, reactions to stresses caused by patients' adjustment to problems associated with early childhood or infancy, psychoneurosis, depression, or anxiety. The first may be considered the equivalent of those which we know as traumatic neuroses, whose etiology would reflect stress which affects the child in circumstances in which he feels helpless, unable either to fight or flee.

It appears best to avoid drawing any such conclusions prematurely. It is useful to begin by assuming that when someone is said to be sick, whether by him or herself or others, no matter how the complaint is couched, his or her overall well-being is diminished. It follows that those thought to be sick are in some discoverable, objective ways different from those not thought to be sick. These differences, however, are by no means necessarily of a "health" nature as measured by cosmopolitan medicine. Rather, the presentation of a complaint simply indicates that something is amiss; the problem may just as well be located in social relationships or relationships with spirit beings as in the sphere of disease. As White (1972:18) has put it, "we can . . . proceed safely on the assumption that something must be the matter with a patient who consults a physician when in fact nothing is the matter with him."

We assume that the difference between those who are and are not suffering susto may be located in one or more of three systems of the self—social, psychological, and organic—and that stress affecting one of these systems may be wholly or partly transmitted to others "so that several become involved in the process of adaptation and defense" (Caudill, quoted by Cassel et al. 1960:940). From this perspective, interaction among physiological, psychological, and sociocultural processes produces variations in relative health. This model has the advantage of assigning no greater weight to problems of, for example, an infectious nature than to a discrepancy between an individual's expectation and actual performance or to problems produced by maladaptive emotional responses.

We further assume that each individual has an ideal level of well-being, or homeostasis. We do not suggest that anyone ever achieves this ideal; rather, it represents a standard for evaluating actual health status. As Howard and Scott (1965) comment, "equilibrium, conceptually, is merely a postulated state toward which the organism may tend, but which is never fully attained." We see stressful forces generated within the sociocultural, biological, or psychological environment as calling for the expenditure of energy by the individual to maintain well-being. Because the three environments are open to one another, what taxes one environment will exact energy from all three. Ordinarily, the individual's energy is sufficient to the demand. Sometimes, however, the demand exceeds the supply, and the overtaxed individual may develop such symptoms as headaches, joint pains, disturbed social relationships, emotional crises, and others. The forces that tax a person's energies will henceforth be called *stressors* (cf. Mason 1975:29), and *stress* will refer to the effects they are presumed to have on the individual. Stress here is similar to State III in Selye's classic description of the General Adaptation Syndrome (1956) and is equivalent to what Scott and Howard have called "tension" (1970:272–273). Several hypotheses derived in part from previous research on social stress phenomena guided our efforts:*

1. Susto will appear only in social situations that victims perceive to be stressful.
2. The social stresses reflected in susto will be intracultural and intrasocietal in nature. Stresses occasioned by conflict between cultures or by an individual's cultural marginality or social mobility (in other words, the frustration or alienation that

* For excellent reviews of social stress research, see Dohrenwend and Dohrenwend 1974; Levine and Scotch 1970; Levi 1971; Lazarus 1967; Mason 1975; Selye 1975. Our approach to social stress has been most influenced by the work of John Cassel and collaborators; Holmes and Masuda; Wyler et al.

often results from relations with members of a social stratum distinct from that into which one has been socialized) will be symbolized by problems other than susto.

3. Susto will appear as a consequence of an episode in which an individual is unable to meet the expectations of his or her own society for a social role in which he or she has been socialized.

Corollary A: Because these societies differentially socialize males and females (see O'Nell 1969; Rubel 1964), and because society's expectations of male and female children differ from those held for mature men and women, it is expected that girls and women will be afflicted by susto as a consequence of experiences different from those which jeopardize the health of boys and men of the same society. For example, girls are socialized to be demure, dependent, and home-oriented, whereas boys are trained to show aggressiveness, independence, and orientations toward occupational and public-responsibility roles. We would not expect many girls or women in these societies to manifest susto as a consequence of inability to meet male-gender responsibilities. Neither should one expect a young man to suffer ill effects from his inability to carry out successfully a task usually assigned to women.

Corollary B: Since these three societies attach greater importance to the successful accomplishment of some tasks than of others, the more importance socializers attach to a particular task, the greater the likelihood that susto will occur in association with failure to perform it adequately. It follows that, although females and males both risk illness as a consequence of failure adequately to perform sex-specific and age-specific tasks, not all such tasks are equally risky.

4. Although all persons in these societies believe in the concept that vital essences leave the body and that distress accompanies such an occurrence, not everyone will actually fall victim to this kind of problem. It is hypothesized that individual personalities act as contingency variables. That is, if

two members of a society matched for age and sex fail to meet adequately the society's role expectations, one may respond to his self-perceived inadequacy by becoming asustado, whereas the other may adapt by an expression of generalized anger or by displacement of hostility. Moreover, among those who do become asustado, the severity, chronicity, and frequency of episodes will vary systematically with respect to personality and societal variables.

Uzzell (1974) looked carefully at some of the earlier work on susto and arrived at a different explanation from this one for its occurrence. He suggests that the victim of susto assumes a "sick" role primarily in order to impose his or her definition upon situations and thereby control the interactions. "This implies dissatisfaction with existing definitions but it does not necessarily imply 'role stress' or perceived inadequacy to meet the demands of a role" (p. 374). Instead, Uzzell concludes, "asustados take time out, relieve themselves for a time of some of the onerous tasks they are obliged to perform." We will return to Uzzell's persuasive argument after presenting the findings of this study.

Since we declined to make any a priori judgments as to the nature of susto (although we did not initially expect it to be associated with either organic or psychiatric difficulties), we had to devise ways of measuring dimensions of social role, organic disease, and psychiatric impairment, each independently of the others (cf. Mason 1975:24). We created three original measures to do so, one to assess the level of social-role stress, the others to measure severity and gravity of disease. In addition, we adapted to our needs the standardized 22-Item Screening Score for Psychiatric Impairment. The procedures for the development of each of these tests and their evaluation prior to adoption are fully discussed in later chapters.

Although victims of susto reach back in time for one or several traumatic events to explain their conditions, we considered it likely that susto reflected the cumulative effects of fairly long-term debilitation resulting from social problems with which the victim was unable to cope (e.g., problems in relationships with spouse or with provision for family), which exacted energy from the emotional and biological dimension as well. The assumption that derives from the open-system model is that a response required by one such dimension may tax resources in one of the others (Cassel et al. 1960; Howard and Scott 1965; Mechanic 1962:4–5; Selye 1975:39, 41).

Although we might have carried out this research in a single community, the conclusions would have been limited to that unique cultural setting, requiring replication in other groups. The ethnographies we have cited demonstrate the presence of susto in different Hispanic cultural settings, creating the opportunity to build on earlier studies and to determine whether the social attributes of a person co-vary with susceptibility to the condition regardless of cultural context. To what extent do circumstances leading to becoming asustado override cultural differences? This was our guiding question. Efforts to answer such a question have been relatively uncommon in anthropology, in no small measure because of the tradition of anthropologists' working in a single community rather than comparing several. If, in fact, affliction with susto did regularly co-vary with characteristics of victims in different cultural and social settings, it would appear to be a shared response to similar social stressors within a particular range of sociocultural contexts.

In summary, this is an effort to discover the meaning of an "exotic" health complaint by showing how those who complain of susto differ from those who do not. The chapters that follow specify the procedures we used and their results.

2

The Samples

THE similarity of previous ethnographic accounts of the susto phenomenon from regions highly diverse in cultures and languages made it reasonable for us to think that a causal explanation transcended cultures. However, to test our hypotheses in only one society would leave us with concern that the results might not apply to other societies, even within the same cultural and language group. Consequently, rather than test them in only one group, we worked in several with different histories, languages, and cultures. This procedure offered the possibility that the results would provide some understanding of human behavior that transcended social group or culture (see Eggan 1954:748). Furthermore, we felt an "hypothesis worth testing once in a field situation deserves replication both in that and other settings" (LeVine 1970:193).

It was critical to ensure that institutions such as the form of government and gender-specific role expectations were similar in the various societies because, if they were not, we could not be certain that we were observing a relationship between the same social forces and susto susceptibility. Likewise, we already knew from our own experiences, and from observations reported by others, that an agent, like a Catholic priest or a schoolteacher, can have a marked influence on villagers' thinking about supernatural forces, or what they believe to be the "appropriate" ways to comprehend illness. We therefore selected societies that shared the same experience in regard to change-agents. The critical consideration was that the communities be comparable, not whether such persons were present or absent.

The features of the three communities we sought most assiduously to control were demography, income, gender-role expectations, form of governance, and the influence of important outside change-agents, such as Catholic priests, schoolteachers, or physicians. In addition, the variables with which we sought to differentiate these communities were maternal language and cultural heritage.

One of the communities is Valley Zapotec in heritage, and all residents speak the Valley variant of the Zapotec language. Another is of Chinantec heritage, in which the Dzah-hmi dialect is spoken. The third population (also Valley) is of Ladino, or mestizo, culture, and its population speaks only Spanish. This latter group has been mestizo—or non-Indian—for at least the past two centuries.

The communities are clearly distinct from one another both geographically and historically. In this respect, J. W. M. Whiting has advised:

> A simple precaution is to avoid using two cases which are known to have derived from a common origin within the recent past. That is, within such a short time that their cultures have not had a chance to change. A more cautious rule would require choosing no more than one case from a linguistic area in which the languages were still mutually intelligible. (1954:528)

There is little risk that their separateness was contaminated by "Galton's Problem," as we shall try to show. Neither ethnographic nor ethnohistorical information suggests significant direct contact between either of the valley groups and the Dzah-hmi Chinantecs. Moreover, there is little direct contact between the two valley communities despite geographic proximity.

There can be no doubt that the maternal language—Spanish—of the Mestizos derived from altogether different roots from either of the two indigenous languages. The latter were also derived from different language families—the Zapotec language forms part of the Oaxaqueña group and, according to what

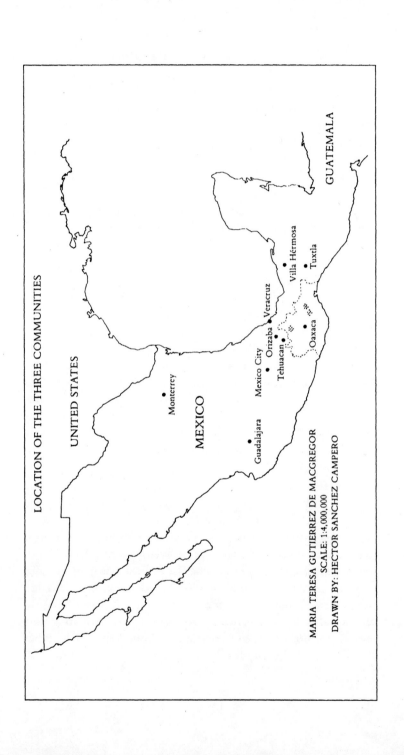

LOCATION OF THE THREE COMMUNITIES

UNITED STATES

GUATEMALA

MEXICO

Monterrey

Guadalajara

Mexico City

Orizaba · Veracruz

Tehuacan

Oaxaca

Villa Hérmosa

Tuxtla

MARIA TERESA GUTIERREZ DE MACGREGOR
SCALE: 1:4,000,000
DRAWN BY: HECTOR SANCHEZ CAMPERO

Swadesh concluded from lexicostatistical testing, the Chinantec language lies outside that group, separated from it by at least 5,000 years. Even more, Swadesh's evidence (1967:96) suggests Chinantec is so different from languages of the embracing Macro-Mayan network as to recommend its being placed entirely outside that Meso-American affiliation. Although Dzah-hmi groups of Chinantec, and Sierra Zapotec-speaking people have enjoyed social and economic contacts for a very long time, Valley Zapotec is a different language from Sierra Zapotec. It is possible that there has been meaningful cultural contact between these highland Chinantec and Zapotec of the valley, but there is nothing to suggest that theirs has been a relationship in which the culture of one has strongly affected that of the other. Providing support for such an impression, Swadesh concluded that ". . . Chinantec appeared to be a long way from Zapotecan as long as it was compared with the Isthmus dialect, but proved to be not nearly so remote from that of Ixtlan [Sierra]" (p. 87).

The separateness of the roots from which these groups drew their cultural nurturance is testified to by Driver's work (1974). He concluded that when populations living close to one another speak different languages it can be predicted that they will also have distinctive cultures. That finding receives support from genetic data that testify to the inconsiderable levels of intermarriage that occur between these highland Chinantecs and their Zapotec neighbors (Zavala et al. 1980).

Our effort was to conduct a quasi-natural experiment to the extent possible, varying certain critical characteristics (i.e., language and culture), and attempting to hold others (e.g., gender-role expectations and form of governance) constant. All three groups were peasant by nature, and lived by dint of subsistence gardening, supplemented by small-scale production of produce and/or manufactured goods for local markets. In the best sense of the phrase, they represented part-societies (Redfield 1956). In all these localities, the major crop was maize, grown almost entirely for household consumption, and supplemented by other crops grown primarily for the same end.

Two of these communities—the Mestizo and the Zapotec—
were located in the Tlacolula wing of the Valley of Oaxaca. Due
to its moderately high elevation, approximately 5,000 feet above
sea level, and the protection offered by adjacent mountain ranges,
the climate of the valley tends to be cool and dry. Rainfall is not
copious, with a yearly average of approximately 26 inches, the
heaviest falls being registered in September. Soils vary even within
the same community. Except for rare patches of bottomland
alongside rivers, none of the soil in this area is of first-class
quality, ranging between lands of second or third class, and those
whose utility is restricted to the gathering of firewood and the
foraging of goats and sheep. These second- and third-class lands
are cultivated with the aid of simple wooden plows drawn by
uncastrated bulls.

In contrast, the Chinantec group lives on lands extending from
the highest range of the Sierra Madre del Sur—Sierra de Juarez—
down to approximately 2,000 feet above the sea; the head-town,
or *cabecera,* is found at 6,000 feet above sea level. These lands
range from alpine in the upper reaches, whose natural cover is
pine forest, down to rain forest, which represents the northern-
most extension of the great Central American tropical forest.
Although many of these Chinantec lands are covered by pine
forest and boulders, and are too cold to be productive, others
are quite fertile and exceedingly well watered. The highlands
depend on seasonal rainfall and are cultivated with the aid of
wooden plows drawn by bulls; in contrast, the tropical lowlands
are wet throughout the year, are cultivated by the digging stick
and, although very fertile, provide but one crop of corn a year
because the constant cloud cover prevents sufficient sunlight
from getting through.

The three populations range between 800 and 1,800 with the
Mestizo group the smallest, the Chinantec the largest, and the
Zapotecs in between. Although numerically there is considerable
disparity between the largest community of 1,800 residents and
the smallest with 800, population density per kilometer is virtually the same. The Chinantec *municipio* evidenced a density of

28.22 persons per square kilometer as compared with 30.0 per square kilometer in the other two groups (*IX Censo General de Población, 1970, Datos Por Municipios, Cuadro I*).

All three populations are governed by a political system in which male members are obliged to fill administrative posts without salary. They represent variations on a theme of the traditional Meso-American civil–religious hierarchy. Each has responded in somewhat different ways to the emigration of adult males, and to the directives that emanate from state and federal governments. A man suffers strong social pressure to give his time, energy, and money to the public well-being by his service in the local governmental structure.

The positions a man fills become increasingly demanding of his time and money as the years progress. The higher and more responsible the position, the greater the personal expenditure of cash and goods by an office-holder. For example, a person who sponsors the fiesta honoring the patron saint in the Mestizo pueblo expends a relatively enormous amount of money and produce, whereas among the Chinantecs the person occupying the office of *Presidente Municipal*—highest of the secular posts— is obliged personally to pay the costs of his numerous official trips to the state capital, together with the costs incurred by those officials who accompany him. These duties at the top of the pyramidal structure are onerous and costly, so it is not surprising to find nominees for these positions—and their wives— reluctant to accept nomination. Nonetheless, social pressures to accept are remarkably powerful, and failure to meet those expectations is labeled socially undesirable. The only way to avoid the opprobrium heaped on those who fail to accept office is by leaving the community entirely. At the time of the study, this was a feasible alternative only for the Mestizos. On this matter, Corbett commented that:

> . . . the likelihood of migration decreases motivation among young men to serve in municipal office. It seems unproductive to invest time and money in civic participation when it will serve no long-term pay-off. (1974:40)

None of the three communities is rent by persisting structural opposition. Despite the fact that the Ladinos are currently divided into three barrios and the Chinantecs formerly had four such divisions, there is no evidence that these currently exert strong influence on the self-identification of residents, or on their relations with residents of other barrios.

Other indications of status serve to differentiate among residents of the Chinantec and Ladino pueblos. Among the Chinantec, individuals known as *caracterizados* are influential in decisions of importance to the community. Caracterizados are adult males who are literate in and have a command of the national language, and who are credited with the capacity to think through difficult problems, especially those which have reference to relations between the community and forces outside of it (e.g., the federal or state governments, the timber companies, or neighboring communities). Although many of the caracterizados have passed through the hierarchical civil–religious structure, attaining the respected status of *ancianos,* some of them have not. Theirs is an advisory role to the Presidente Municipal (see Dennis 1973) and his officers, much as the group of ancianos serves in an advisory capacity to the municipal officers. Although some of those known as caracterizados are among the wealthier men of the community, there is no correlation between that status and their relative wealth. Nor can it be reported that this group of influentials is in any way self-perpetuating, passing their status on to sons or nephews.

Among the Ladinos, ownership of milk cows and the manufacture of cheese for the city market is profitable enough to contribute to the formation of a segment of the population that is considerably better off than others, and socially influential. Reflective of these wealth differences are a dozen locally owned pickup trucks, and one passenger auto. Since the introduction of electricity in 1969, television sets, refrigerators, and a few electric pumps to obtain water for household use have appeared. These innovations are so recent as to have begun with the current generation of middle-aged residents. They derive from increased access to the city with the arrival of the Pan-American highway in the 1940s. The influential townspeople are characterized by formal schooling ranging from two to five years, with a mean of three and a half years; however, their schooling is little different from others of less influence. Their newly acquired status seems more closely related to an ability to exploit the few resources available, and to turn them to good advantage by commerce with the city.

Furthermore, among these Ladino influentials there seems to have developed a consciousness of like interests, and a growing social distance between them and those who have been less entrepreneurial. Although the criteria for identifying "leaders" among the Ladinos resemble those used to identify caracterizados among the Chinantecs, the former seem to have developed a greater sense of like interests and separation from others than is true of the caracterizados. The Ladino influentials seem to act in a more cohesive fashion, being linked among themselves by godparental and other bonds. Nonetheless, governing structures in both towns encourage, even require, universal participation by males in public service, with the greatest responsibilities currently assigned to those boasting the greatest literacy in Spanish.

The extensive lands cultivated by the Chinantecs and the logistics dictated by seasonal cultivation in distinctive ecological settings have led to the presence of several concentrations of population, of which the largest by far is in the head-town with a year-round population of approximately 600. Smaller numbers of people reside in hamlets constructed alongside the Sierra highway, which was completed in 1956. A few people live all year round in some of these hamlets, but most divide the year between their hamlet residences and their homes in the cabecera, or head-town.

In the three sample communities, access to cultivable lands is the minimal feature of a reasonable life. In each, small privately held properties are important and are passed by inheritance from fathers to sons, more rarely to daughters. Access to arable land is the economic base of a family's existence, but it also serves to confirm that a man is a citizen with rights in the community, and obligations to its continued well-being—that he is an *hijo del pueblo*. Although all sons theoretically have reason to expect a share in heritable private holdings, in truth it most often passes to the youngest son in the expectation that he will assume responsibility for his aging parents as they become unable to care for themselves. For similar reasons, the parental home is usually assigned to the youngest son as a form of social security for the parents who expect to be able to remain under its protective roof. Although this appears the best insurance for enfeebled parents, it is not at all a strategy that encourages confidence, and many families suffer severe trauma, persisting for many years, as the parents attempt to make tactical decisions regarding distribution of private holdings and residences in order to ensure care for themselves in their declining years. Indeed, among the Zapotecs, there are instances of widows retaining rights to land they hold in trust so as to guarantee continuing support from waiting sons.

The importance of heritable private land and homes is such that, apart from its influence on relationships between parents and children, it often has a divisive effect on relations between brothers. Among the Chinantec, competitiveness among brothers is often severely exacerbated by unequal distribution of their father's private properties. In addition, here and among the Ladinos, private holdings are complemented by other properties, title to which rests in the community.

These publicly held lands among the Chinantec are communal in nature, community title dating from early colonial or precolonial eras. These communal lands, the forests they bear, and the produce of certain fruit-bearing groves, are controlled by a political and social entity known as *Bienes Comunales*. Bienes Comunales is an association composed of native-born males whose ancestors are credited with wresting their gardening plots from virgin forest. The association elects its own officials, and votes on legislation governing these properties as well as to how profits from their exploitation are to be used. For example, the highland timber is harvested by lumber and pulpwood companies, which contract with Bienes Comunales as to the number of board feet they will be permitted to cut during a contract period, how much the companies will pay per board foot, where access roads are to be built by the companies, and the scale of wages paid *comuneros* who fell and prepare the timber prior to cartage.

Any matter that affects the cultivation of communal soil, or the rights to its use, is a matter for decision by the membership of Bienes Comunales, not the municipio. However, the memberships of Bienes Comunales and the municipio overlap to a great extent, even though there are a few individuals who work only private lands and do not have rights in communal holdings. Another indication of the interrelationship that obtains between these autonomous entities is provided by the fact that the few men from other municipios who marry into Bienes Comunales families gain access to arable lands by performing *cargos* (duties) in the public service hierarchy.

In contrast, publicly held lands among the Ladinos are not a reflection of the fact that they have been worked since "time immemorial" by this community. Rather they represent an award in 1937 by the agrarian reform agency, based on the need for land of these previously landless peasants. These lands were expropriated from a large hacienda for which they had labored, and were awarded in trust to the community of which they were members. These *ejido* (public) lands are worked in small lots by peasants who are members of an ejido organization, which legislates their use. Although all members of the ejido are also members of the community, not all members of the community belong to the ejido or have rights to its lands. Despite the fact that both Ladinos and Chinantecs may have rights to the use of lands title to which rests in a public entity, the communal lands of the Chinantec are far more extensive than the ejido holdings of the Ladinos.

Cultivation of the land and, in particular, the back-breaking tasks involved in transforming it from a wild to a cultivable state, is primarily a man's role. In all three communities, cultivation is impossible without plow animals. Uncastrated bulls are the animals of choice, and these are very expensive. A man without bulls must, therefore, rent them from a neighbor, or give part of his harvest to the owner from whom he rents them. An exception to this is found among those Chinantecs gardening in the tropical lowlands, where machete and digging stick are the only tools required. However, in all these groups, the often long distances between fields and home make desirable such draft animals as horses, burros, and mules. They literally take the load from a man's back and are much prized possessions.

It is not uncommon for women, particularly from the poorer families, to work in the fields. However, women's tasks are of a lighter nature than their menfolk's. Similarly, unmarried men work with their fathers, and under their supervision, the more difficult tasks falling to the more mature of the men. The most onerous work is done by hired day-laborers, those whose lack of land, illness, or other misfortune forces them to work for others.

A youth reaches social maturity at the time of his marriage, regardless of chronological age. On marrying, he becomes liable to community labor—*tequio*—clearing paths, building roads, or doing other construction work, as ordered by the local authorities. Marriage also initiates his career in public service, where he will hold office well into his most vital years.

A girl does not attain social maturity until she has borne viable children within a stable union. In the Indian groups, a woman's relative immaturity will continue in marriage, if she resides in the household of her mother-in-law, until one of her own daughters provides a grandchild, product of a stable union.

Uniformly, having children is positively evaluated and encouraged; it represents one of the foundations of a successful union. A union which has not produced offspring is considered problematic and inherently frail. Children validate their parents' union, add to the household's productive labor force, and promise social security for their parents in declining years.

In a union without offspring, it is the woman on whom the

blame is placed. A mother must also breast-feed each of her children and failure to do so makes her a subject of opprobrium.

In these groups, there is a clear differentiation of gender-roles. From infancy on, boys and girls are socialized differently and, among the Chinantecs, midwives charge a family twice as much for the delivery of a boy: a male will earn twice as much as a girl, they point out. That is a realistic expectation since males earn considerably more than their sisters throughout life. They are able to command higher wages as agricultural hands, and possess many more opportunities to move to more lucrative employment in Mexican cities, or in the United States.

These differential expectations for males and females are reflected in the extent to which boys and girls are encouraged to pursue formal schooling. When our current generation of middle-aged subjects was of school age, there existed far less opportunity to attend primary school, much less the secondary grades. At best, these towns provided schooling up to the fourth year, and it was decidedly rare for a pupil to leave home in order to pursue secondary education in an urban school. As late as 1970, in the Ladino town, the one best served by public transportation, costs of attending secondary school in the nearby capital were so great that only three adults had gone beyond the primary grades, all of them men (Corbett:40).

Chinantec girls are dissuaded from continuing to the secondary level since they will not "need" such training in order to be mothers and housewives. "You are not going to serve as a town official," they are advised. This differing emphasis on formal schooling is reflected in distinctive levels of literacy and, within the Indian groups, command of the national language. Thus, few Zapotec girls at all attended classes prior to 1960. By 1965, however, the local school population more faithfully represented the sex ratios of school-age children. Nonetheless, of ten children attending secondary school in the city, only two were girls. Yet today, these Zapotec women, as well as the Zapotec men, take great pride in being literate.

Among the Chinantecs, criteria for awarding respect to men

and women more clearly reflect differences in educational expectations. A man earns little respect if he does not have a good command of Spanish, and even less if he is illiterate, whereas a woman may command respect even though she is not literate or proficient in Spanish language skills.

Among the Mestizos:

> In the school census taken in 1970–71 . . . only three percent of the adults admitted to being illiterate. . . . These figures are no doubt deflated due to embarrassment involved in admitting illiteracy to the school teachers (who were the census takers). Illiteracy suffers severe negative sanction. Some who are listed as literate in the census admitted privately that they could not read or write, but answered affirmatively to avoid shame. (Krejci, 1974:32)

Similarly, the school census of Zapotec pupils taken in 1965 listed 170 adult illiterates, of whom 150 were women. O'Nell surmises that those figures grossly *underestimated* the illiteracy problem, though not necessarily the disproportion between the sexes. Clearly, in the 1950s when our sample was attending school, these towns provided little opportunity to proceed past the fourth grade, and boys received far more encouragement to remain in school than did their sisters.

Throughout those years, our sample attended primary grades, and teachers resided in each of the three locations. These teachers took active roles in introducing social and cultural change, and perceived themselves as mandated by the national government to recommend and implement forcefully radical social, cultural, and economic changes. In a number of important ways, these resident schoolteachers have exerted strong influence in each of the sample communities.

Although the three populations are Catholic in faith and training, none boasts a resident Catholic priest. Religious celebrations and sacramental acts must await the periodic visit of the parish priest, unless families go to churches in other communities.

Except among the Zapotec, other religions did not gain a

foothold until the late 1940s. At that time, only about five percent of the Zapotecs identified themselves with evangelical groups. Then, some residents, vociferous in their opposition to the use of hard-earned resources for the celebration of traditional religious feasts—especially sponsorship of the *mayordomias* (celebration of the saints)—found a sympathetic hearing from outside evangelical missionaries who were periodic visitors. Today, most of those Zapotecs who are not practicing Catholics identify themselves as Seventh-Day Adventists. In the early years of that movement, membership in an evangelical cult separated adherents from other residents, since the former did not serve in important community roles celebrating the saints. This no longer represents a problem because, in 1950, the town authorities, supported by a significant proportion of the citizenry, simply decreed that mayordomias and other religious services were no longer obligatory. Although religious service became voluntary in 1950, secular service to the community remained an obligation, a distinction that has continued.

The municipal government exercises formal control with its local police, and derives its power from the consensus support of the citizens. Even more pervasive and of greater influence are the informal means of governance, both human and supernatural. There are social norms and, when someone has transgressed one of these norms and is stricken by an infirmity or other grave problem, the difficulty is commonly attributed to the transgression. This is another form of governance. Above all else, the good citizen—man or woman—is the one who lives tranquilly, at peace with his neighbors. To live at odds with one's fellow beings, to bear rancor, to be argumentative, to be clearly self-serving and selfish, grasping and uncooperative, will call into play not only verbalization of the transgression by one's neighbors but sanctions exercised by supernatural beings.

At individual and community levels, every effort is made to avoid disagreement and, considered much worse, open confrontation over differences of opinion. Consensus is sought at all costs but, failing that level of agreement, differences are played down, and the rhetoric of being "a united pueblo" becomes overriding. A commentary in the municipal archives of the Mestizo town provides a good illustration. Although acquisition of a water system ensuring potable water was of high priority to the community, the plan recommended by government engineers remained unapproved and unimplemented for a full six years because it would have provided residents of two barrios easier access to the hydrants than residents of the third. A substitute plan was finally developed that provided for more equal access to the hydrants for the entire community. The archives note, as follows: "Not to take that potential problem [unequal access] into account could well generate divisiveness between us, causing many problems. What we most ardently desire is always to work together in a unified manner."

With respect to the decision to host a full-time physician among the Chinantecs, a matter we know to have been controversial, the following interview segment is relevant.

"Following 1958, then, little by little the government began to pay some attention to the needs of the community. So that in 1972 it began to provide a physician. The matter of healing began to undergo changes; prior to that time healing had been in one's own hands. It was the new highway which made the difference."

"Were you in favor of bringing a physician into the community?"

"Oh, yes! We were all in agreement."

"You were all in agreement? In other communities the elders have opposed the arrival of a physician."

"No, no. Here, thanks be to God, a unified front has always been present. Everyone united. Everyone together, a consensus, here it has always been that way."

Similar commentaries about potentially divisive problems and ways of resolving them by avoiding fractiousness are found throughout the field notes.

3

Description of Susto

As indicated in the previous chapters, social norms are enforced by indirect sanctions at least as constraining, if not more so, as the police power of the municipio and state. The most often apparent of these is sickness, which is considered a social sanction. Sickness is attributed to both the initiative of supernatural forces and to the manipulation of such forces by evil humans, who are thought to be witches.

An individual who becomes symptomatic seeks alleviation but, at the same time, searches for possible reasons why he or she has become ill at that particular time. Individuals are understood to vary considerably in their relative susceptibility to sickness: some are strong and, consequently, resistant, others weak and susceptible. The very young and the very old are inherently weak—the former have not yet developed resistance, the latter are in the process of losing it. In addition, women are considered weaker and more susceptible to sickness than men. Within each of these groups it is recognized that some individuals are relatively stronger than others. Thus, it is assumed that, when two individuals of the same sex and approximate age are exposed to the same noxious circumstances, one may succumb and the other may not. Those differing reactions are regularly observed and noted by the people. The differences are explained by the fact that the one who succumbed was simply less resistant than the others: "Her blood is weaker." Traditional specialists—diagnosticians and diviners—are able to predict who is weak and more susceptible and who is strong and more resistant by the way in which a person's blood courses through his body, a determination made by pulsing, or "reading the blood," "listening to the blood," "consulting the blood." Furthermore, reading the blood through pulsing at the wrist enables a curer to determine the relative gravity of a patient's condition.

In instances in which a patient is neither very young nor of advanced age, and has enjoyed relatively good health, symptoms cause considerable preoccupation. If the patient fails to respond to the treatment called for by the diagnosis, concern is heightened. There is then the possibility that he is suffering the consequences of an inadvertent slight or affront to a supernatural being or, and of equal seriousness, he is a victim of someone else's malevolence. Fear of exciting someone else's rancor is a powerful contributing factor to the effort to live at peace—*en tranquilidad*—with family and neighbors.

Such understandings are part of a comprehensive explanatory framework by which occurrences of illness are explained. In this view, illness—lack of well-being—derives from the loss of vital bodily substances such as blood, semen, heat, or the essence known as *alma* (soul). The other immediate cause of illness is attributed to the intrusion of a foreign substance or substances. Prominent among these substances are spirits or their representations in the form of *aires* (winds, breezes) as well as insects, worms, or such objects as twigs, pebbles, and tobacco smoke, which are forced into a victim's body at the behest of a witch.

Good health is equated with systemic harmony, or homeostasis. In a healthy body, balance is characterized by the even distribution of "hot" and "cold" humors. Anything that would disturb that distribution should be avoided. Potential sources of disturbance include (1) the wandering or displacement of the "soul," womb, fontanel, or nerves, (2) a rush of heat, cold, moisture, or powerful emotions, too strong or too sudden to allow the body to re-equilibrate on its own, (3) failure of either normal or diseased body fluids to drain completely, since self-cleansing is essential for equilibrium.

Symptoms indicate that balance has been disrupted by internal or external stressors. They further indicate what must be done to restore equilibrium. The steps taken to restore balance vary according to the imbalance perceived. They usually require administration of herbs, foods, or other substances to neutralize the imbalance: purgatives to unclog offending organs or orifices, and the use of a live chicken, turkey, or other instrument, which they brush over the patient to "sweep out" an intrusive substance and absorb it. Clearly, these are not the only concepts with which our sample people confront illness, but they do form the ideology to which such new ideas as the effects of bacteria and the efficacy of antibiotics are adapted.

Ideas about the prevention and curing of illnesses logically flow from these explanations. Individuals are careful to avoid excessive loss of bodily substances, but when this proves unavoidable they "replenish" them as rapidly as possible. Strong emotions are avoided, and precautions taken to avoid rancorous social relations, which may incite another to direct invasive magic against an offender. Finally, care is constantly taken to prevent qualitative changes in the humoral balance of the body: to avoid becoming too "cold" or too "hot." When homeostasis is lost, the victim is administered herbs and minerals that contain the needed "qualities" in the proper amounts. Likewise, sickness attributed to loss of vital essences is cured by recalling or replenishing them. Foreign materials intrusive to the body are drawn or swept out by magical means, usually by ritual specialists. It is within this general frame of health and illness that we will discuss susto, one of the most prevalent of all those illnesses of which these people complain.

Susto is a well-recognized entity with a well-established etiology, diagnosis, and regimen of healing. Although understanding of susto varies among villages and even among residents of the same village, the consistency across otherwise distinctive cultures is most impressive. There are some exceptions, among which are the nouveaux riches among the Ladinos in this study who currently deny the reality of susto as a problem. Some case materials follow to illustrate the reality of susto in these three societies.

When residents of the Ladino village heard the report that a middle-aged neighbor had committed suicide, "an epidemic of sustos resulted among relatives and neighbors." One of those who was *asustada* (*asustado* for males, *asustada* for females) was Elena, an elderly aunt of the suicide, a widow who, even prior to her husband's death, had been quite poor. She now owned insufficient land and had to launder the clothing of others in order to support herself. Elena had borne nine children, of whom seven had died in infancy and an eighth at the age of 20. Her remaining son was mentally retarded with a serious drinking problem, causing Elena considerable anxiety. She acknowledged herself to be held in low esteem by her neighbors who considered her a gossip who "sweeps the dirt from the streets with her long skirts!" On one visit to the anthropologists, she commented, as she wiped her face and eyes in exhaustion, "I have suffered so much, and have had so many sustos."

Another instance from the Ladino village should be mentioned because it clearly outlines the circumstances under which susto (the condition) can be expected to occur. Our ethnologist was pregnant at the time, and her husband was gathering data in another village. Heavy rains threatened to bring down a roof under which the family automobile was parked, requiring her to move the car. After she accomplished this, a neighbor suggested she be given a simple preventive cure for susto, both for her own sake and that of her unborn child.

The helpful neighbor went home and returned with a bottle of *mezcal* (an alcoholic beverage) and proceeded to spray Jean's chest and back with the cold liquor, causing Jean to gasp from the shock. Over the next few days, other neighbors brought gifts of eggs, tortillas, and cheese, suggesting that, if she did in fact develop susto, she would not be able to or would not want to engage in her normal cooking activities.

Two Zapotec cases follow. The first refers to a woman who devoted her time primarily to the care of her husband and their only child, a boy, and secondarily to the manufacture of pottery ware for commercial sale. On one of her weekly trips to market, the heavily laden burro—carrying all her pottery—repeatedly fell to the ground, eventually smashing the entire load. There is no indication from her account that she felt in any personal danger from the awkward animal, nor is there any indication that she suffered explicit repercussions from her husband, although the financial loss to the family was considerable.

One year following the incident, she reported herself suffering from susto, which she attributed to the earlier event. In the year elapsing between the loss of her pottery and the initial complaint of susto, several things had occurred. Most important of all was that she had twice become pregnant and twice suffered spontaneous abortions. She expressed a fear that she might never conceive and deliver another viable child. Her concern over her son increased and became a constant, gnawing fear. She and her husband both explicitly expressed a desire to have more children, but the miscarriages had increased their doubts that they would attain that cherished goal.

A neighbor of theirs explained his own susto condition as a result of recently coming upon a dangerous snake ensconced in an *arroyo* (dry gully). He reported being startled, but he could recall no sense of fear until he attempted to kill the creature, only to discover it had disappeared as suddenly as it had revealed itself. His was a short-lived fright, however, and he forgot about it in his preoccupation with other matters on the walk home.

A few weeks later he felt ill enough to consult a physician. The resultant treatment availed him little and, since his discomfort continued unrelieved—in fact he thought it worsened after that treatment—he consulted a local *curandera* (healer). During his meeting with her, she probed for events in the past that would serve to explain his problem; they agreed that the encounter with the snake was of importance and that he was suffering susto due to that frightening experience.

To understand this man's problem in full context, one must be aware that, prior to and following the incident with the snake, he had bought a lot and had begun to build a house on it. However, due to his failure to ensure that he held clear title to the plot, he was forced into long litigation, risking loss of his investment in both the land and the newly constructed house. We will return to this case shortly.

In another case, a wife was subject to constant accusations that she was not as responsive to her husband's needs as a wife should be, and that she was also negligent in the care of their modest home. One evening, after berating her once more for her inadequacies, her husband went out. She resolved to wait up for him and, when darkness enveloped the reed structure of the house, she lit a kerosene lamp to serve a double purpose—to keep her awake, and to light his path home. She grew increasingly sleepy with the passage of time, but he still did not appear. She refilled and relit the lamp, and decided to hang it from a hook in the ceiling.

She was determined to stay awake, but she leaned against one of the reed walls, and promptly feel asleep. As she slept, the lamp shifted position on the hook and slipped to the side of the wall where she reclined. She was awakened by the flames, which not only licked at her clothing but were beginning to engulf one wall of the house. At that moment her husband made his appearance and, between the two of them, they beat out the flames. She was not burned badly, but one entire section of the residence had been destroyed. She was terribly frightened by this calamity and became asustada. The husband used the accident to confirm his earlier accusations of her negligence.

During our research, a woman described a susto that had occurred to her in 1939. This Chinantec had been traveling at that time from the fields back to her home. She and her companions were beginning to ford a swift-flowing river when she lost her footing and fell in the water—"me empujó el rio." The current started to sweep her away, but her companions were able to reach in and pull her out, senseless and soaking wet. Someone loaned her a blouse until her own clothes had dried out.

Immediately after her rescue she had "felt asustada." She suffered only a loss of appetite at the time, and did not lack energy or motivation to carry out her customary duties until three years later, in 1942, when her *matriz* (uterus) began to pain her. Field notes record her account: "Immediately after the accident in the river she felt a loss of appetite; however, she did not then feel a loss of motivation in carrying out her usual role tasks until the susto illness was joined by the matriz illness, both together putting her out." At the time of the cited interview, 32 years after her *susto del rio,* she was suffering from *three* sustos and a hemorrhaging condition, which she attributed to a "loosening" of the womb—"se aflojó la matriz." The second of her three sustos had occurred as a result of encountering a snake, and the third occurred as a consequence of looking on while one man killed another in one of the hamlets where she worked.

Three months prior to our visit, her condition had taken a decided turn for the worse, and for the ensuing three-month period—day and night—she had lain on a sleeping mat at home. She was unable to sit up for more than ten minutes at a time, as was made evident during our visit. She complained that when she did sit upright, her spinal column hurt. While in a standing position, her womb ached. Whenever she climbed the hill, she lost her breath; her breath no longer "circulated." When she worked much in the house, or walked uphill, her spinal column hurt. Even while lying down it hurt her. Now she had no appetite and when she did eat something, she was unable to keep it down. "She does not want to do anything, nothing at all in the house. A hired woman does everything; when she eats tortillas, they taste like chicle." Medical examination by Dr. Collado revealed a large, though probably benign, uterine tumor. Surgical intervention was strongly recommended, but rejected as unfeasible by the patient and her father.

On another occasion, the husband of an asustada woman sought consultation from the anthropologist. He and his wife had one child, a boy. They very badly wanted a larger family, but during the nine years following the birth of their son the wife had suffered seven miscarriages. She was presently pregnant, and was terribly concerned that she would again fail to carry the fetus to term. She was suffering from a serious susto, which had occurred some years before. The husband informed us that she was one of those individuals who, ever since childhood, show themselves to be weak and easily asustada. (Clinical examination of his wife found that she suffered palpitation and breathing difficulties subsequent to physical labor. Her blood pressure and pulse were normal, although she complained of a buzzing in her ears. She complained of generalized pains and weakness, and a bad taste in her mouth, swelling of her feet, and nightmares. Varicosities were detected, and laboratory results indicated the presence of two classes of parasites, and a slight anemia. Despite all of this, the pregnancy concluded happily, resulting in a healthy boy.

Then there was the case of Rogelio, a Chinantec who vacillated between calling his problem *muina* (repressed anger) and acknowledging it as susto. When interviewed and examined in 1971, Rogelio was 57 years old. Nine years earlier he and one of his two sons had been part of a force that had engaged in battle with a neighboring municipio over a piece of land (see Dennis 1976:176–177). During the attack, the son had been killed and it had fallen to Rogelio to carry his body back to their home village. He was very sad at that time, finding himself left with only one other son, and a daughter who lived in Mexico City. He lost interest in his work and in living, he wept frequently, and felt himself to be weakening physically. According to Rogelio, his health had taken a decided turn for the worse a year before he came to our attention. One day in 1970, he felt a generalized pain and "a burning in his heart" [pointing to his right abdominal area]. This was precipitated by an effort to lift a sack of corn to his back. As a consequence of these difficulties, he had consulted a physician who advised that he suffered "liver problems" for which he was then treated. He later suffered a bout of diarrhea and worsened; he lost his appetite, his entire body swelled, and he lost *la fuerza* (power, strength).

Additional ethnographic information indicates that his remaining son was so drunk and disorderly on one occasion (in

November 1970) that the municipal police placed him under arrest. He succeeded in escaping only to be recaptured and placed in jail. He refused to pay the fine assessed him by the municipal authorities because, he claimed, someone had stolen some of his personal possessions while he was in custody.

Consequently, the authorities removed him from jail and incarcerated his father, Rogelio, in his stead, as the responsible head of the household. Rogelio languished in jail for two days and two nights, suffering intensely from the cold, and from mortification. When he finally agreed to pay his son's fine, he was released. By then he felt "very weak and, more than anything else, very, very sad" ("muy triste, muy, muy, triste. Otra vez me asusté"). He had suffered another susto.

Later, in 1971, while pasturing his draft animals, a drunk began shooting capriciously in the area where Rogelio was working, some of the bullets landing quite close to him. Thinking himself the target, he hid behind some bushes, and again suffered a susto. He attributes the seriousness of his present condition to the combination of three sustos.

His incapacitation continued and a prominent local healer was consulted. We observed his efforts to erase any doubts as to the nature of the problem; he diagnosed it as susto and wasted no time in beginning procedures for curing it. He directed the family to have a number of items on hand for him when he returned that night. These included a bottle of mezcal liquor, a small bottle of *catalán*—another liquor—a cross made of blessed palm leaves, an embroidered image of a saint, cigarettes, leaves of the tarabundí tree, resin, and one of Rogelio's shirts. We were invited to watch the proceedings.

That night, after dark, the curer waited until there were no further sounds from either revelers or the usual passel of dogs. He then stepped outside the house carrying all the articles with the exception of the catalán. The sudden barking of dogs persuaded him to go back inside until it was absolutely quiet; he waited another twenty minutes, and then ventured outside once again.

In the garden, the curer took the bottle of mezcal and shook it vigorously, allowing some to fall to the ground as a libation. He prayed to the spirits inhabiting the area who might have been responsible for capturing Rogelio's vital substance. After finishing several stanzas of prayer in which he called Rogelio's name, in an attempt to retrieve Rogelio's vital substance, he threw a cigarette to the ground, as an offering. He turned to face in a different direction, and repeated the procedure in its entirety. When he had faced in four directions, each time praying, throwing a cigarette to the ground, and calling to Rogelio's vital force, he took the patient's shirt, shook it to its full length, and then rolled it up again.

We then walked slowly and deliberately back to the house, where he lit resinous coals in the waiting brazier, moved the brazier next to the prone patient, and unrolled the shirt in which were the palm leaf cross and the embroidered image. He drew the shirt through the heavy clouds of smoke to waft them over the face and head of the reclining patient.

A tea of nine herbs was prepared and the patient instructed to drink it, as well as some of the catalán. The weakened condition of Rogelio can be estimated by the observation that he was unable to come to a sitting position unassisted; after his wife and son had pulled him to an upright position, his wife scurried around behind, placing her back against his to support him while he sipped the tea.

Finally, the tarabundí leaves were wrapped around his feet (it was later discovered that these were for another of his health problems, not directly related to his susto condition). The wife, the son, and the daughter, who had been called from Mexico City because of her father's grave condition, were all advised to watch the patient closely. No one was to sleep that night if the cure was to be effective!

The healer made arrangements with the anthropologist to look in on the patient early the following morning. (On leaving, the anthropologist was convinced that he would never again see Rogelio alive.) However, he certainly was alive the following morning, although not much improved. The curer explained the lack of improvement with the observation that someone in the family must have fallen asleep. We could look in on Rogelio in the early evening, which we did. He remained unimproved. The healer counseled that no one of those watching over the patient was to fall asleep or the cure would come to naught.

On the following morning, the patient showed signs of a slight recovery and asked for coffee. He seemed to be somewhat more energetic, chipper, and better oriented to his surroundings. The following day was marked by a relapse in which he was as lifeless as on the day treatment had begun. However, following that one-day relapse, he began a slow recovery, regaining his animation and strength a bit more each day. By the end of the third day of recovery, he was walking about the house with the aid of a cane, going outside the house to relieve himself, and talking with others.

Several months later, on returning to the village, the anthropologist wrote the following observations:

> Today saw Rogelio, our patient. He is not only walking about and visiting with neighbors, he is all smiles and laughs, recognizing full well that he had been, in his words "ready to deliver up the account."
>
> He now boasts a good appetite and says that when he was very grave, but on his way to recovery, they fought the good fight ("hicieron la lucha") and obtained four chickens, one of which he ate entirely by himself, the others he shared. He reports having eaten "like a coyote." Even now he is hungry at noontime and again by 3:00 in the afternoon, and he eats tortillas, beans, some meat if he can find it. Also, they have bought some canned condensed milk (a luxury) which he mixes with his coffee.

Several days following that encounter, we found him working in a road construction crew. His job was to wield a heavy steel tamp to crush stone into gravel. Asked how he felt, he smilingly talked about his newfound strength and stamina.

Between the time of the curer's ministrations and his seemingly complete recovery, he was examined by the project physician. The following is from that clinical record:

> Pale and thin, he showed little interest in what was going on around him. Hypotensive—80/50—with a rhythmic pulse of 85 per minute. Heart sounds were without alterations. He complained of a pain in the right hypochondrium, but no other observed pathology.

The laboratory reported: ". . . hemoglobin of 10.1 gr.% with 4.2 million red blood cells per milliliter, hematocrit was 35%, and no evidence of parasites."

Rogelio was one of those asustados who subsequently died; we remain uninformed as to the cause of his death.

Several cases of susto have been presented in varying degree of completeness from each of these culturally different populations. In each instance, there was an understanding by the people involved that the victim had lost a vital part of himself or herself, and that that vital part was recoverable if appropriate measures were taken. Although the term most universally used in Spanish for this vital part is *alma,* which has reference to the Christian concept of soul, use of this term for all three of the populations now seems inappropriate, for reasons that follow.

Among the Chinantec, a victim is understood to have lost a vital substance (called the bi^4 in that language),* which is held captive by spirit forces of the locality where a startling event has occurred. The bi^4 is referred to by several Spanish glosses: *fuerza, voz, respiración.* It is often described as something that oozes or slips from a victim's extremities, such as the fingers or toes. The bi^4 is different from the other vital substance, which departs the body at the time of physical death. This latter is known as the $mmi^2\ gi^2$. In this differentiation between the two vital substances, the bi^4 of these Dzah-hmi Chinantecs is quite similar to conceptualizations of other Mexican indigenous groups, the *zaki* of the Otomí (Dow 1975), and *iwigara,* derived from "iwi, the word

---

* bi^4 is a phonetic rendition of the word used in Chinantec.

for breath" among the Tarahumara Indians (Kennedy 1978:129).

The Zapotecs with whom we were working seemed not at all clear as to what is lost when a person suffers from susto, nor did they appear particularly concerned about its identification. As in the other two groups, a diagnosis of susto is derived from discussion of the symptoms and whether the patient, or members of the close family, can recall an occurrence or circumstance that could be called a susto from any time in the past. The duration of the time that has elapsed between the presumed startling event and the onset of symptoms is not of significance; what is required is some past event that will provide etiological support for a diagnosis of susto. Once such a diagnosis is made to everyone's satisfaction, it is assumed that a vital substance has departed the body, and that patience will be rewarded when identification is made of the event that precipitated its loss. It is not at all co-incidental that in all three communities a critical segment of the curing procedure is to call the name of the patient, sometimes followed by the admonition, "Come back, come back!" Thus, "Juliana, Juliana, come back, come back! Come back, Juliana!" In the Valley Zapotec language, an asustado person is described as *es̱ píṟ it gon sá wě 't* ("the spirit wanders outside"). However close they appear, the Zapotec word /es pír it/ and the Spanish /espíritu/ do not share a cognitive meaning. The word /espirit/ also has a different referent form, /e yai ni/, which brings to mind another vital substance without which a person cannot live and which, as a matter of fact, leaves the body when a person dies. This latter, /e yai ni/, appears more akin to the Christian concept of soul than what departs the body following a susto episode. In view of these apparent differences between the referents to which the Zapotec /es pír it/ and the Chinantec /bi⁴/ apply, and the soul concept, which the Spanish word /alma/ brings to mind, we will henceforth use indigenous terms when discussing the susto condition in these groups. Marcus and Flannery offer some historical depth to this issue:

> At the root of all sixteenth-century Zapotec classification of the
> world was the concept of pèe. Variously translated as "wind,"

"breath," "spirit," or "ánima, lo que da vida," pèe was the vital force that made all living things move and thereby distinguished them from nonliving matter. This was probably a very ancient concept, for it is shared not merely by other Otomanguean speakers, but by less closely related Mesoamerican peoples. (1978:57, 59)

In both Zapotec and Chinantec societies, a person's vital force is dislodged from the body and held captive by spirits, which are associated with the natural environment. Such spirits may reside in a river, or in uncultivated parts of the mountains and forests. They are associated with lightning bolts, fish, birds, and distinctive species of animals (cf. Marcus and Flannery 1978:58). Indian understandings of the causal sequence precipitating susto is that somehow the victim has had unwarranted contact or has caused some affront to one of these beings. Although the element of fright (or being startled) is always present in the people's accounts of events to which susto is attributed, probing uncovers that it is not the fright itself, nor is it the person, dog, bull causing the fright that captures or holds captive the essence of the victim. Although a person will attribute her susto to the fright she sustained when a dog suddenly rushed at her, the bi[4] is not held captive by that dog, but by spirits of the locale in which she was frightened. Entreaties and libations are offered to the spirits rather than to the animal that frightened her. This is easier to understand in a case in which the fright is precipitated by a natural phenomenon other than a domesticated animal or a person. For example, two women were sleeping at home in one of the Chinantec lowland hamlets when lightning entered through one window of the house, traversed the length of the residence, and left through another aperture. Both women suffered a susto as a result. Clearly, in this instance, as in the previous illustration, there is a frightening aspect, but in the latter episode there is present some unwarranted, even undesired, contact with a natural phenomenon. In this case, it is the *cause* of the fright which, affronted, takes control of the vital substance of the person who has transgressed, and to which propitiation must be offered for its return (cf. Bahr et al. 1974:65).

In the Mestizo community, causes of susto are much less liable to be natural phenomena; they are more oriented towards interaction with other persons, or with those animals which form part of the domesticated sphere of the human world. Disagreeable and startling interactions, like being accosted or "breathed on" by a drunk, lead to *susto del borracho;* being startled by a barking dog can lead to *susto del perro;* sparring between draft bulls can bring on *susto del toro.* Since these kinds of causal events are also important for the Indian samples, they may possibly represent a Ladino overlay on an indigenous conceptualization of what happens when a person breaches the bounds separating the human from the superhuman world. We are aided in understanding this difficult concept by reading the excellent discussion of "ways" and "strengths" among the Piman Indians, as presented by Bahr and his colleagues (1974:69, 73, 131–132).

It is not fruitful to attempt to understand the people's explanations of causal sequence in sickness events by imposing those classic models which have proved so helpful in the development of biomedical understandings of disease (Snow 1936; Panum 1970). Concepts of predictable incubation periods (the length of time that will ensue between exposure to an infected person and the onset of symptoms) have been critically important to the logic by which we understand infectious disease processes. As these susto case materials show, the temporal factor confuses, rather than clarifies, understanding this condition if one assigns it importance.

In the illustrative case materials, victims clearly assign susto causality to a startling experience that anteceded the appearance of symptoms. It is particularly noteworthy that in some of these cases—many more could be cited—there is a lapse of weeks, even years, between the precipitating event and the subsequent onset of symptoms. It is instructive to note that the woman who suffered the consequences of the awkwardness of her burro did not report symptoms of susto until more than a year after the loss of her pottery.

The woman with the uterine tumor explained her incapacitation by a susto that had occurred more than 30 years before and by the complications of two additional sustos that had occurred during the ensuing years. When Rogelio was asustado in 1962, he became very sad at the death of his son, although there is no account of a susto syndrome until after his own incarceration in the local jail eight years later. His emaciated, weakened, and unmotivated condition was attributed to those two events, complicated by the susto del borracho caused by the capricious firing of a rifle near him. There occurred a notable interlude in these cases between the complaints of sickness and the events presumed to have precipitated them.

Similarly, the case of the Zapotec man who encountered the snake only to lose sight of it immediately afterwards is instructive. He did not acknowledge symptoms diagnostic of susto until several weeks after the event. O'Nell (1975) has calculated that, for the Zapotecs, the time lapse between a blameworthy fright and the appearance of symptoms ranges from "immediately" to "about seven years." As the case of the Chinantec woman attests, it is not unusual for the range to extend to 30 years.

The presence of susto symptoms may, however, lead to ambiguous interpretations. Although the symptoms are explained as the result of loss of the victim's vital substance, the substance may be gone either as a result of a frightening event *or* because it has been captured by a witch. To label the absence of well-being as susto requires the telltale symptoms together with a plausible antecedent causal event, and treatment is then directed to recalling, or retrieving, the victim's essence. On the contrary, attribution of the symptoms to someone's malevolence results in a different diagnosis and other procedures. When bewitchment is the cause, treatment includes threatening the culprit into desisting from his or her infamous behavior.

Diagnostic procedures are often complex, subject to negotiation; they do not always lead unerringly to a single, unambiguous resolution. To illustrate that point, the process by which a 62-year-old Chinantec man was diagnosed will be presented in some detail. He complained of a loss of weight, sleeplessness, lack of appetite, loss of vision, and general malaise. The curer's initial conclusion on the basis of the symptoms alone was that he suffered problems inflicted by witchcraft. "The head is infected" because the patient was engaged in a dispute with another. "There is a dispute, there is disagreement, *envidia* (envy) witchcraft is involved." The healer then confronted the patient, asking him whether it was not true that he was in dispute with another; the patient denied the finding. The curer then reaffirmed that an argument was the cause of the health problem, whether or not the patient accepted it. "He doesn't admit it but *I* say that he is having troubles with another and, even if he will not admit it, that is what is behind his problem."

Throughout this exchange, he continued bathing the patient around the eyes, face, scalp, temples, forehead, and jaw with a ball composed of herbs heated in the hearth fire. He advised the patient and his wife that the husband was to be bathed on the following day with the same kinds of herbs. In addition, flowers selected from floral offerings left in the church were to be included. After the bath, all these flowers would be used to concoct a tea for him to which sulfadiazine was to be added.

On the day the wife was to bathe her husband, however, the healer read his pulse and arrived at a new diagnosis. He found the blood to be circulating slowly, suggesting that he was "nervioso." The curer ascribed this condition to an aire or sprite that had entered his body when he was already suffering from susto. He asked his patient to tell him about the event that had caused his susto, not whether or not he had ever suffered a susto. The patient responded that "it must have happened four years ago when I and my wife were crossing a river near our ranch in "hot country." They were crossing the river by way of a fallen tree branch when the makeshift bridge broke in two. The force of the break hurled the wife to safety on the far bank, whereas the husband had to save himself by grabbing hold of an overhanging branch and walking hand over hand to safety.

Although his wife confirmed that account of the mishap, he denied that he suffered susto as a result. Although he repeatedly denied suffering susto as a result of the accident, the healer repeatedly reaffirmed the diagnosis. The fright, or *impresión fuerte* (strong impression) suffered by his patient permitted penetration of his eyes by the aire (representing the spirit of the river), which eventually caused his loss of vision.

What has just been recounted illustrates the negotiating process by which a diagnosis is sometimes arrived at, permitting appropriate treatment to begin. The account is colored by the fact that this particular healer is one of the less well thought of diagnosticians in the community; also, it is the only occasion on which a diagnostician was observed insisting on the correctness of his diagnosis. Nonetheless, in this, as in other diagnoses of susto, a past event evoking an impresión fuerte, or fright, was obligatory.

Furthermore, there are cases in which a person has suffered a mishap that *could* have given rise to susto, but has not yet. Preventive measures are often engaged in. In one instance, parents carrying a baby to their cornfield sat down on the ground to rest. When they rose to continue their journey, they picked brush with which to beat the ground at the place where the child had reclined, requesting the earth spirit not to retain the child's bi[4].

Other constant features appear in reports of patients suffering susto. Evidence consistently appears that a victim is experiencing particularly taxing problems that call into question his or her capacity to fulfill expected roles adequately. The cases of the two pregnant women, one of whom suffered seven miscarriages, the other having experienced two over a brief period, serve to illustrate. In each of these instances, both the woman and her husband desperately wanted more children and, in each case, the woman expressed pessimism and strong anxieties about her capability to carry the fetus to term.

Returning to the case of the man who saw the snake and then immediately lost sight of it, we know that a period of several weeks elapsed between that incident and his report of symptoms. During and prior to that period, he was suffering the consequences of having risked his own and his family's fortunes in a questionable property deal in which they stood to lose everything. In the course of litigation, it was implied that he had acted imprudently in risking family resources and, vis-à-vis his role in the society at large, he appeared somewhat foolish, even irresponsible. At worst, he appeared to some as possibly dishonest in what they believed was his attempt to take advantage of an unclear situation for his own gain. The family with which he was in dispute perceived him to be and gossiped about him as though he were a conniving and unscrupulous person, an accusation of very serious consequences in this group.

In sum, there are a number of constants that characterize these case materials. The communities' explanation is that a startling or frightening experience leads to a loss of a vital substance or force: alma among the Ladinos, bi^4 and es pír it for Chinantec and Zapotec, respectively. In the first group, the substance is wandering, and a cure requires that it be induced back in to the victim's body, whereas in the two Indian groups it must be freed from its captors, and then induced back into the body. There is no specific time period between the precipitating event and the appearance of symptoms. The only requirement is that such an event precede the onset of symptoms. Finally, symptom onset appears to occur during particularly trying times for an individual, a period in which he or she is undergoing stresses associated with negative self-evaluation about role performance.

4

Sampling of Groups

IN terms of the major criteria established prior to selection of the communities, our samples have fulfilled most of our expectations. Although the Chinantec population of approximately 1,800 persons is considerably larger than either of the other two, the much larger territory of the Chinantec makes the population density of all three virtually identical. In contrast, our expectation that the selected communities would evidence little social stratification was less satisfactorily fulfilled. Although there are no significant differences in levels of formal education, we were surprised by the relative wealth brought some members of the Ladino group through the commercial production and sale of cheese. This unexpected and uncontrolled-for difference affected the distribution and, probably, the number of acknowledged cases of susto among the Ladinos. Furthermore, it came as a surprise to learn of the social stigma which Chinantec men attach to susto. We assume that this stigma had an impact on the number of men who would agree to appear in our experimental sample and, as commented on in the discussion of disease findings, it very likely had its effect on the severity and gravity of the illness admitted by those Chinantec men reporting themselves asustado.

Thus, there are surely more cases of asustado men, and the cases of women are probably underreported, owing to factors we failed to foresee in the sociocultural process by which individuals are labeled as sick.

Other than these unexpected difficulties, it proved both feasible and productive to test these hypotheses in a framework in

49

which selected social, demographic, and economic features were controlled across the three societies which, at the same time, varied in their respective cultures and maternal languages.

Once we had selected the communities for our study, our next procedure was to find asustado individuals, or people who believed they were suffering from susto. A community may sustain a belief in susto and have specialists in its diagnosis and care, but it is always an individual who experiences susto. Ultimately, therefore, the experiences of individuals reveal the events in which susto can be examined.

Our sample was therefore composed solely of persons complaining of susto at the time of fieldwork, or of those willing to concede to the opinions of their relatives or of curers that they were victims of the condition. The effort to identify victims was rigorous. It depended primarily on native procedures for labeling persons as asustado.

Inclusion of an individual in the sample depended on local opinion, either personal or consensus, and not on a judgment of the researchers. This fact had important, if unexpected, consequences for the composition of the sample. We realized during later phases of the study that native labeling criteria had probably skewed the sample in the Chinantec and Ladino communities. In the former, the relatively few men in the sample was in part due to the idea that to complain of being asustado was an admission of being "womanly." The case of Rogelio, described previously, will illustrate the point.

We had gone to interview Rogelio on the recommendation of his first cousin, a woman, who labeled him "asustado." On arriving at his house, his lack of well-being was immediately apparent. During that first interview, he claimed his condition was due to muina—a choleric but repressed anger. When we later encountered the cousin, she asked us what Rogelio had said. When told "muina," she burst into paroxysms of laughter. Finally, noting the ethnographer's chagrin, she explained between gasps, "The men here are so funny! Because they think it unmanly to suffer from susto, they prefer to call their problem muina!"

A different idea influenced our sample of asustados in the Ladino village where people with higher incomes and social influence acknowledged its reality but felt that belief in it was a sign of ignorance and superstition. The Krejcis wrote:

> Whereas in the past, susto was an accepted form of behavior for any villager, by 1972 it was becoming less so, particularly among the more affluent villagers. Although still experienced among the poor, it tended to be kept private and/or secret. Those who experienced susto suffered in two ways, first in the debilitating effects of the illness and, second, in the refusal of the changing society to provide support, sympathy, and adequate means of curing. (Krejci and Krejci 1981)

Nonetheless, a sample was constructed that included proportionately fewer of the nouveaux riches than others.

The asustados formed a group against which to test the research hypotheses. To select a control group as much like its counterpart as possible, we used three criteria. First, since asustados are by their own definition "sick," their controls must also consider themselves "sick," although not implicating susto in their condition. To admit only individuals who thought themselves sick into the research samples served as a comparative control over the entire sample since "sick" persons were compared only with other "sick" persons. The control group was drawn from patients presenting complaints at the free clinics provided the several communities by the project, and clinic records documented the necessary biographical data. A second criterion matched males with males, and females with other women. The differing life situations, social roles, and biological processes of men and women required this procedure. The third criterion was age. Again, life situation, role expectations, and biological processes obliged controlling for this factor.

We sought to match as nearly as possible one control for each of the asustados. Such matched pairs were established *only* within the same community, so as to control for culture and language, too. Matches by age were not exact because many people could not give the year of their birth and, in some cases, we could not identify a clinic patient of exactly the same age as an asustado in need of pairing. When more than one person was equally appropriate to match an asustado, selection was made randomly.

The sample was susceptible to treatment in the following ways: (1) each asustado could be compared with a match, (2) groups of asustados and controls could be compared by gender within cultural groups (e.g., male Zapotec asustados with male Zapotec controls), (3) asustados and controls could be compared by gender across cultural groups, (4) asustados could be compared with controls without regard to gender (e.g., Chinantec asustados with Chinantec controls—this last was made possible, in part, by making ratio adjustments to take into account the difference in the number of questions men and women were asked on the Social Stress Gauge), and (5) groups with susto in the various communities could be compared (e.g., Zapotec women and men with susto could be compared with similar Ladinos with susto).

In several tests, the size of samples used varied slightly. These variations were the result of: (1) use of part samples (or subsamples) of the data, which were more directly relevant to the question being asked, (2) the full use of the data approach for statistical tests on small subsamples, (3) a rare instance when information on an individual was incomplete. For example, a mother and daughter refused to give blood samples alleging that, since their susto had weakened them, drawing blood would weaken them still more. In this instance, we could not include them as members of samples being tested for disease symptoms, nor could we use this information from the two women who served as their matched controls. However, because we did possess their scores on the social-stress and psychiatric-impairment measures, they and their matches were included when these measures were tested. These procedures were dictated by the small size of the subsamples, which required conservation of maximum data for statistical testing.

Methods of Testing the Hypotheses

In addition to traditional ethnographic approaches, the salient aspects of our investigation were: operationalizing the measures, developing and utilizing samples, and testing data from the samples statistically to determine the probabilistic nature of the findings. Each of these is discussed in turn.

Susto patients were identified as (1) individuals complaining of being asustado, (2) persons under treatment by a traditional healer who identified the problem as susto, regardless of whether the patient was fully convinced of the diagnosis, (3) a person whose discomfort was at a subclinical level, although agreeing with others who labeled him or her as asustado. Following O'Nell (1972), the level of severity—discomfort—played no role in the selection procedures.

Hypotheses and theoretical constructs derived from ethnographic data led Rubel (1960) to formulate the conditions associated with susto. Later he (Rubel, 1964) formulated a series of hypotheses about the association between susto and self-awareness of inadequate performance of critical social roles. Subsequently, O'Nell and Selby (1968) tested and confirmed one of those hypotheses. These efforts, together with an unpublished pilot study, paved the way for developing the Social Stress Gauge used in the present research (O'Nell and Rubel 1980).

Symptomology was operationalized in accordance with conventional procedures of clinical medicine. A panel of two physicians developed diagnoses and other assessments, having no other information about the patient than that generated by the clinical protocol. The following information was collected on 100 patients: symptoms and complaints, personal medical history, family medical history, results of a physical examination by a project physician, and results of clinical laboratory analyses of blood and stool. As already noted, two women declined to give blood, although all other clinical information was available for them.

Patients' health problems were diagnosed by the panel of physicians and classified according to *The International Classification of Diseases,* 8th edition, World Health Organization. Further, the overall clinical picture of each patient was assessed on the basis of two scales developed by Collado for relative severity and gravity.

Psychiatric impairment was defined and operationalized by adopting the 22-Item Screening Score for Psychiatric Impairment. Procedures by which this particular measure was selected, and its adaptation for use in Oaxaca, are described in a following section.

The psychiatric impairment measure consisted of a single score representing an accumulation of points awarded on each of the separate items. Higher scores were assumed to reflect higher levels of psychiatric impairment. However, no score, whether high or low, was assumed to reflect any fixed level of impairment.

The tests of our hypotheses consisted mainly in attempting to determine whether the numerical patterns in the results were consistent with expectations. We were interested in the nature and directionality of the values, and the magnitude they attained. We expected to find either a divergence in which the numerical values differed from one another, or a convergence. We were always interested in the directionality of divergence. That is, did the numerical values form predicted patterns? In certain of the measures, we expected asustados to attain scores differing from those of the controls, and the differences to point in a certain direction (i.e., that asustados would score relatively high and their controls relatively low).

Ultimately, the most important question was the *magnitude* of difference or association once the pattern emerged. Magnitude is the probability or likelihood of occurrence of a given statistical value. Different events have different probabilities, which can be determiined statistically. The probability that a young, strong, and healthy villager would awaken in the morning after a night's rest was high; the probability that he or she would inherit five million pesos was low.

Because no one expects to predict events with 100 percent accuracy, and correlations may occur simply by chance, expectations were limited by a specified margin of error. We established a 5 percent margin of error to indicate whether hypotheses received support or confirmation. That is, we considered a hypothesis to receive support from the data when a numerical value was received that would occur by chance less than 5 percent of the time.

Most of our hypotheses were constructed to predict the pattern and magnitude of the outcome. Although each of us entertained somewhat different expectations, the major hypotheses were tested in ways designed to prevent biased results.

Levels of Social Stress

We predicted that persons suffering susto would concurrently perceive themselves to be inadequately performing crucial social roles. The discrepancy between their expectations and their performances was presumed to cause them stress. Since all human beings experience some degree of stress, whatever their society or situation in life, we had to address the question of relative levels of social stress. Levels vary by individual differences in accommodating to stressors, and by differences in what is perceived as stressful. Individual differences in potential levels of accommodation are probably largely genetic, and therefore basically physiological (Selye 1974). In contrast, individual differences in what people perceive as stressful are largely due to processes of enculturation.

If stress occurs frequently in human experience, it is reasonable to assume that individuals develop levels of tolerance to it. Stress in excess of this accommodation level will be felt as distress. McGrath (1970:18) refers to variations in tolerance levels as underload and overload stress.

If it were possible to assess tolerance levels for an individual, one could establish a scalar point at which stress becomes distress. We attempted to get at variations in what individuals thought stressful by virtue of being socialized into traditional gender-roles of their societies. Caudill, in one of the first anthropological efforts made to find out how an individual's culture and interpretations of stressors mediate response to them, commented as follows:

> Such questions are directly related to what may be perceived as stress in a particular culture or society. A certain event may be a stress for one individual but not for another; such an event may be interpreted very differently in the context of a particular culture, compared with that of another; and such an event may have different consequences, depending on the type of social structure within which it occurs. (1958:10)

A Social Stress Gauge was developed to gather data on the social expectations, perceptions, and performances of these sample individuals. The aim was to test associations between levels of stress and whether individuals included susto in their health complaint. We predicted a positive statistical association between the scaled measures of social stress and presence of the susto condition.

The Social Stress Gauge has three parts (see Appendix:127). The first part, the Social Factors Questionnaire, was developed for use as a record sheet in the field. The second part was designed to code data gathered in the field, and the third part was a score sheet to tabulate judgments.

Our earlier field experience in Mexico, and literature from the culture area, were used to construct this instrument. In earlier ethnographic research, Rubel and O'Nell had observed numerous circumstances that could be identified as stressful to those experiencing them. Through detailed discussion of these observations with townspeople, we arrived at a tentative list of situations that would probably engender social stress in the groups with which we expected to do research.

Grouping potential areas of social stress for adults in rural Meso–America, we arrived at a set of four categories:

1. Living arrangements, especially housing and the adequacy of residential quarters
2. A person's opportunities to develop an appropriate gender-role
3. Abilities and dispositions to accept and respond to role expectations within the family
4. Abilities, dispositions, and opportunities to accept and respond to role expectations outside family, but within the community.

A pilot study to test the validity of these categories was conducted in the Zapotec community in the summer of 1969. That effort supported the validity of the four categories and suggested that one category could be predominant over the others. That is, a person might show high stress scores in one category, with low scores in the other three. Furthermore, the pilot study confirmed the wisdom of alloting different weights to potential stressors. This possibility had been anticipated some years before:

> Since Hispanic–American societies attach greater importance to the successful accomplishment of some tasks than of others, the more importance which socializers attach to a particular task, the greater the likelihood will be that susto will occur in association with failure to perform that task adequately. (Rubel 1964:281)

One of the more important things to grow out of the pilot research was a discovery that the subjective, interpretive judgment of a respondent undergoing stress is critical information. The individual's cognitive assessment of the situation, in other words, may make it more or less stressful. Another researcher of stress phenomena commented: "There is little doubt that the existence of a causal link between life events and illness makes theoretical sense only when considered in terms of the meaning of life events for particular individuals." (Brown 1974). Although we identified role performances that were important to members of the three societies, we did not feel equipped to get at the cognitive interpretations of individuals speaking different languages and with different cultures, to say nothing of their unique experiential histories. We were seeking differences between groups of people, those with susto and those without, rather than the personality differences among individuals.

While instrument construction began before the ethnographers initiated fieldwork, modifications continued during early phases of fieldwork prior to the use of the instrument. The gradually paced development of the field instrument permitted its testing for administrative feasibility and reliability under actual field conditions. During its development, the gauge was not tested with people subsequently included in our samples. Only after it had assumed its final form was it used with sample individuals.

The Social Factors Questionnaire was used by the ethnographers and their assistants with each person in our samples. It was initially translated into rural Spanish, and tape-recorded. Then it was transcribed on tape in the appropriate Chinantec and Zapotec dialects by bilingual members of those groups. Translations and transcriptions were checked for conformity with their meaning in the Spanish language instrument by having community members who were not included in the samples respond to the taped transcriptions before they were used with sample respondents. Separate versions for males and females were presented to males and females, respectively, since certain items in the Social Factors Questionnaire were designed to elicit gender-specific responses. Responses to the taped instrument were recorded on a copy of the Social Factors Questionnaire by the ethnographers and their field assistants. For the majority of items, the respondents were required to state their opinions or preferences and then indicate at some later time their actual behavior. For example, a woman is asked early in the process: "If someone from this community works for another person for wages, is this an appropriate thing to do, is it just all right, or is it unfortunate? Later, the same respondent is asked: "Have you worked as a wage laborer for someone else during the past two years?" Certain questions were asked to determine respondents' perceptions of adequate performance in their roles, with follow-up questions to discover their assessments of success or failure in actual performance. A copy of the questionnaire is available. (Appendix:127).

A panel of four coders was selected to code and score the materials gathered by the Social Factors Questionnaire after all data had been collected and we had returned from the field. Coders were selected from applicants unacquainted with the nature of the hypotheses and unfamiliar with life in rural Mexico.

The coders were initially instructed on the use of the instruments with simulated field protocols. With two to four hours of instruction and practice, each of the coders achieved the desired competence in the use of the instruments. Intercoder reliability between two persons working on the same protocols ranged from 80 to 100 percent agreement when cumulative social-stress scores were compared. Coders worked independently of one another at all times. Each protocol was scored by at least two coders.

In general, social stress for any set of items in the field instrument was gauged by response disparities indicated by perceived role requirements and perceived levels of role performance. The absence of a discrepancy was scored 0. Moderate discrepancies were scored 1, and maximum discrepancies received a score of 2.

The total social-stress score was determined for each respondent by adding the scores for the item sets. Higher cumulative social-stress scores connote higher levels of experienced social stress; lower cumulative scores connote lower levels of experienced social stress. No effort was made to indicate a critical level of social stress since the scores over the sample as a whole represented only ordinal measures. Since the Social Factors Questionnaire did not cover as many items for males as for females, ratio scores were computed for the cumulative totals to render them comparable between women and men.

Levels of Psychiatric Impairment

Since earlier writers had suggested that a complaint of susto was equivalent to a middle-class person's complaint of psychiatric difficulties (Billig et al. 1948; Gillin 1945; León 1963; Pages Larraya 1967) we wanted to discover whether our susto samples were characterized by more emotional difficulties than the patients without susto.

Several short tests were available to screen psychiatric symptoms within a population. These screening devices had been developed for use in the United States, although some were also prepared with cross-cultural testing in mind. We considered three instruments of this kind: the Health Opinion Survey (Macmillan, 1957), the Cornell Medical Index (Brodman et al. 1956), and the 22-Item Screening Score for Psychiatric Impairment (Langner 1962). The 22-Item Screening Score was adopted because it had already been translated into Spanish and successfully tested among women of rural Oaxaca and Mexico City (Langner 1965). At the time we adopted this instrument, the questions seemed to lend themselves to modification without changing their original thrust, but more difficulty was encountered in their cognitive and linguistic adaptation than we had anticipated. The instrument was oriented to goals similar to our own—to provide "a rough indication of where people lie on a continuum of impairment in life functioning due to very common types of psychiatric symptoms" (Langner 1962:269). While we were adapting it in the field, other researchers were reporting it to be a more adequate test for problems of neuroticism than for psychoses (Crandell and Dohrenwend 1967:1528; Fabrega and McBee 1970:669–673; Manis et al. 1963:108–116; Muller 1972:601; Schader et al. 1971:599).

Another criticism leveled at this screening score was that it was not restricted to problems strictly emotional in nature. In this critique, Crandell and Dohrenwend (ibid.) divided the inquiries of the original instrument into four subsets, of which they considered only one uniquely to address a respondent's psychological health, another to reflect physiological dimensions, and a third the psychophysiological symptoms; a residual subset was nominated as "ambiguous." Working in the United States, they found that scores on the respective subsets varied independently of one another according to the social class characteristics of respondents. Lower-class subjects tended to report higher scores of physiological discomfort, and lower scores on items more psychological in orientation; however, other researchers have not been able to replicate those results (Roberts et al. 1973; Meile and Gregg 1973:648). In the two Oaxaca Indian villages in which we applied the instrument, social class stratification was of little significance. The only one of the three to display sharp stratum differences was the Mestizo group. But here, as was true of the other societies, even the highest social class respondents had attained less than a sixth-grade elementary school education.

The first step in adapting the Langner screening score was to test whether his Spanish version adequately communicated to other rural Mexicans. With the assistance of a Mexican psychologist, Dr. Raymundo Macias, we tested it among residents of a rural community in the State of Mexico. They volunteered to participate and were urged to indicate any difficulties in understanding the language in which a question was phrased, or in comprehension of the response options (see Chance 1962:417). On the basis of their suggestions, several of the original questions were rephrased. Peasants and researchers worked hard to develop more adequate ways of asking the same questions. The effort was to change the form without affecting the basic inquiry. For example, one of the original questions asked, "Do you feel somewhat apart or alone even among friends?" Respondents commented that the word "friends" in this context was overly abstract. The inquiry was modified to, "Do you feel alone even among others of the community?"

Another question that required revision was, "Have you personal worries that get you down physically, that is, make you feel physically ill?" Respondents consistently inquired whether these "personal worries" had reference to family problems, and told us that only such problems were serious. Consequently, the question was rephrased as, "Do problems of a family nature tire you or make you physically ill?"

When we were forced to make a choice between gaining greater comprehension and maintaining the questions in their original forms, enhanced comprehension was the rule in all instances! The modified versions were brought to Oaxaca where bilingual men from the Chinantec and Zapotec municipios were asked to dictate indigenous language versions onto tape. Later, different bilingual men from each group translated the Chinantec and Zapotec versions back into Spanish. Comparison of the original versions and the back translations revealed no significant differences.

The final stage in this adaptation was to have a native speaker in each group read each question slowly and distinctly into the tape recorder, pause for five seconds, announce that he was about to repeat the question, and then repeat it.* Notwithstanding the fact that adaptation of the instrument was undertaken with great care, a subsequent difficulty among the Chinantecs—to be described shortly—emphasizes the problems that are inherent in any effort of this kind. (Problems have been reported by others who have adapted the 22-Item Screening Score for use among different ethnic and social class segments of the United States (Meile and Gregg 1973:648; Roberts et al. 1973:25).

The modified version was administered in a standardized fashion to respondents in their own homes. Each person was advised that we would like to ask some questions while using the portable tape recorder, which was placed conspicuously on the floor, on a small bench in the household, or on the lap of the interviewer. The respondent was shown how the equipment functioned, the manner in which it was turned on and off, volume control, and so forth. Individuals were also advised that their responses would be noted on an answer form by the anthropologist or the interpreter. Following careful explanation of the procedures, a respondent was asked whether he or she had any questions. If there were no questions, the machine was switched on.

---

* Copies of these tapes may be obtained at cost by writing Arthur J. Rubel.

During the first interviews among the Chinantecs, it was observed that notable uncertainty greeted one question, usually followed by an unconvincing "yes." So common was this response that the interpreter was asked whether respondents were encountering problems in understanding what was being asked. Surprisingly, the interpreter answered that the people were having difficulty in recollecting past experiences. The problematic question was: "Do you ever feel so restless that you cannot stay long in one place?" This was a modification from one of the original 22 items: "Do you ever feel so restless that you cannot sit long in a chair (cannot sit still very long)?" The earlier change had been made in accordance with two important considerations: (1) it is most unusual to find a chair in the home of these Indians and (2) respondents during the pilot phase had difficulty in recalling when they were "just sitting still," not eating, engaged in productive work of some kind, or talking with others.

Many of the Chinantecs reside in different ecological zones during different seasons of the year. In the tropical lowland ranches, individual families live in dispersed single dwellings, or in hamlets containing several households. When they come to live in the head-town, much more neighboring and conviviality—*alegría*—mark their lives. Consequently, they understood our question to mean: "Do you ever feel so restless and lonesome for company in the lowland hamlets—after three or four months—that you want to return to the more convivial head-town?" Despite efforts to revise this question, it was unusable among the Chinantecs. Because residents of the Zapotec and Mestizo towns always live in concentrated settlements, they found no difficulty with this question. Nevertheless, to maintain uniformity across groups, it was discarded.

Levels of Organic Disease

The medical investigation of susto had as its goal an apparently simple and easily obtained objective: to determine whether patients with susto were medically sicker than patients who did not have susto. Collado the project clinician, confessed that before this study:

> . . . my medical attitude toward susto was one of curiosity, since I considered it only a psychological problem with negligible organic consequences except in those cases with a long history and inconclusive psychological resolution. It was a bias, inasmuch as I had never examined or treated a patient with susto. I believe that this bias toward this and other folk illnesses is shared by a large portion of my colleagues, and poses a persisting problem in daily practice; this is especially so in instances where the physician is of one culture and the patient of another.

To avoid this bias we developed the following methodology. One of the most conclusive ways to determine whether one group of patients is sicker than another is to ascertain whether, over a period of time and under similar conditions, one group suffers significantly more fatalities. We had hoped that patients would have their problems successfully treated but, for some, their problems ran a course culminating in death. This permitted the calculation of the number of deaths in each of the two samples of the sick, those with and those without susto. These calculations are based on the seven-year period from 1972 to 1979 which followed collection of the illness data.

A central consideration of the theoretical framework was to decide whether the study would focus on the illness encountered in each group, or on the degree to which each person was ill. The advantage of focusing on the illnesses was that it would remain within orthodox medical conceptualization and terminology, which derive diseases from etiology, physiopathology, and pathogenesis. In addition, we decided to include the diagnosticians' holistic clinical impressions in the assessment. By these means we planned to obtain a clearer picture of which of the two groups, the asustados or the controls, had more health problems and were more gravely diseased.

Dr. Collado's clinical premise was that the patient should be fully evaluated emotionally as well as organically. He was convinced that one cannot comprehend the one without the other. With this premise in mind, organic and psychoemotional dimensions were included in the clinical investigation, with emphasis on the former.

Who is more sick, a person whose problem comprises rheumatoid arthritis, a respiratory infection, and contact dermatitis, or one with cancer of the stomach? Measured simplistically by the numbers of signs and symptoms, the first would be adjudged more sick, although the condition of the second is clearly more life-threatening. Although the quantitative aspect could not be omitted, it would also be necessary to find a way to evaluate the level of gravity—risk of death—of each of the groups (and each individual) to avoid a conclusion that "asustados have more problems but we don't know whether this configuration is more or less life-threatening than that presented by the controls."

Even in the best clinical centers, it is sometimes impossible to arrive at a diagnosis of the disease or diseases from which a patient suffers. In the present investigation, the conditions under which we were constrained to evaluate patients were quite unusual—examining sick persons in a dwelling in a small rural community; sometimes completing a clinical protocol with the help of interpreters; examining patients with only the resources of a medical kit and the subsequent assistance of laboratory tests of blood and stool. We weren't very optimistic about arriving at a diagnosis of all the diseases afflicting our patients. Should we take into consideration only diseases successfully diagnosed? What would we do with symptom clusters—syndromes—that hinted at, rather than demonstrated, a disease? Should we include them? We decided that we should because this was the information obtainable through our limited resources. Similarly, we decided to include both symptoms presented by the patient and the signs judged important by the examining physician. We considered the possibility that the level of pathology in asustados might very well be characterized by a large number of diverse and diffuse symptoms, as reported in some ethnographic accounts, so typical of psychosomatic pathology.

The clinical study was conducted in three stages. The anthropologists selected the universe to be investigated, and the physician formulated the framework in which to evaluate health problems, the research instruments, and the guidelines for administering them. In the second stage, the anthropologists brought the patients together, and a physician examined them. In the third, descriptive examinations were evaluated by two physician-scorers who independently assigned to each patient, a level of severity, and a level of gravity.

The instrument used was a simple clinical protocol, with some items specifically developed to measure levels of gravity and severity (see the appended protocol). The protocol was constructed on the assumption that examinations would be done in rural settings, primarily by a fifth-year medical student assisted, in some cases, by an interpreter. In taking a patient's history, communication could be distorted through translation by an intermediary, whereas the remaining portions would be filled in with responses less subject to interpretation and with information from the physical examination. The most objective data were to be derived from examinations (in the clinical laboratory) of patients' blood and feces. Thus, the protocol was constructed to emphasize objectivity and reduce as much as possible bias created by third-party intervention. Further, it was designed to minimize the amount of clinical judgment required of the senior medical student.

It was important that the instrument assess gravity and severity separately. If asustados were simply malingering, a high score on severity would be expected, with low scores on gravity. Conversely, if susto was associated with serious disease, high gravity and severity scores would be expected.

Besides information identifying the respondent, the protocol comprised the following:

1. Four sections: (a) history of the problem, (b) a listing of symptoms and the frequency of their occurrence, (c) the physical examination, (d) laboratory results. This is the information with which a physician customarily arrives at a diagnosis.

2. This format permitted scoring the results mathematically, with the aim of evaluating and scaling levels of gravity and severity. To better understand this, see the scoring sheet and the accompanying instructions that guided the two scorers (Appendix:157).

Identification of asustados (experimental group) and non-asustados (control group) was made by means of a code established by the anthropologists and unknown to the various physicians who performed physical examinations, conducted the laboratory tests, or arrived at diagnoses and scores of severity and gravity. Eight patients mentioned susto as part of their complaint to the examining clinician, but we believe that such information did not affect the overall results.

Whereas the screening score for evaluating mental status and the Social Stress Gauge were translated into the respective indigenous languages, the medical protocol was not. In one society, it was necessary to use a Chinantec–Spanish interpreter, but there is no reason to think that the accuracy of information obtained through this interpreter was different from that obtained in other cases.

The clinician used mimeographed clinical protocols, completing them in customary fashion, during and after the interview. The reverse side of the sheet was used to record additional important information. This strategy increased assurance that the necessary research data were collected from each patient; often this does not occur and protocols are filled in much later.

Laboratory tests were conducted in the city of Oaxaca, in the laboratory of two highly regarded professionals. A stool sample from each patient was examined by means of a concentration technique, in the search for intestinal parasites. A hematocrit analysis, together with counts of red and white cells, was conducted on a blood sample taken from each patient following a period of at least four hours without food. The laboratory followed standard procedures for all blood and stool samples received from patients referred to them by physicians in the city of Oaxaca and surrounding towns. The collection of samples was made with the prior consent of the patients. Patients were given a small plastic container in which to place the stool sample, which they were instructed to deliver to the physician the next day. The physician took the blood sample according to instructions and with equipment provided by the laboratory. Samples were transported to the laboratory in thermos containers; in order to maintain an adequate temperature, gelatinlike material was frozen in a common refrigerator and then placed in the thermos to preserve the blood. The laboratory was consistently satisfied with the condition in which the samples were delivered. The project staff thus succeeded in overcoming problems of transportation, communication, and other logistical difficulties. The only problem encountered was the attrition of two asustado patients (mother and daughter) who refused to give blood samples owing to their "weak state."

Those subjects who were interested were told the objectives of the study: to study susto from different angles and particularly from a clinical viewpoint in order to inform medical schools and practitioners of the findings and, in that way, to contribute to their better understanding, and the resolution, of this health problem. Generally, those who were interested in the study agreed to cooperate "so that physicians may know something about what we suffer from, although they 'don't believe in it.'"

The protocols were submitted to the two general practitioners in Mexico City who made up our scoring panel. The protocols were submitted separately to the physicians, so their diagnoses would be made independently. Except for eight cases in which the susto condition had been mentioned by the patient and written on the protocol, the physicians didn't know to which group patients belonged.

Other physicians (research associates) subsequently classified each diagnosis according to the *International Classification of Diseases*, 8th edition, World Health Organization (table 10).

The same physicians who performed the diagnoses scored levels of gravity and severity for each case, following the appropriate instructions (see Appendix:160).

Seven years after completion of the fieldwork, a collaborator*
collected information from the authorities in two of the communities regarding all deaths that occurred among the sample of
patients; a Chinantec resident did the same in the third community. Neither colleague knew whether a patient on our list had
been an asustado or a control.

Did we measure with our instrument what we wanted to
measure? The cluster of complaints presented by each patient
was noted on the clinical protocol. The medical diagnoses were
based on those descriptive data in the same way that clinicians
customarily derive their clinical diagnoses—that is, based on
communication with the patient, the clinical examination, and
the laboratory tests. The convergence of diagnoses arrived at by
the scoring panel of two physicians speaks in favor of their
validity. The validity is even greater with respect to the laboratory results—a diagnosis from these is even more objective.
With respect to level of gravity, we did not have means by which
to verify whether, in fact, a patient with a high level of gravity
was close to death. Nevertheless, the subsequent results, and
especially the analysis of case fatalities, make us think that the
instrument did indeed measure the gravity of patients' conditions. We cannot assert the same with respect to severity since
there was no mechanism to verify that patients scoring higher
on severity had reduced their customary activities proportionately. In sum, we can state that our instrument was most valid
in the laboratory tests; next most valid in the clinical examination
for quantitatively and qualitatively evaluating morbidity; satisfactorily valid in measuring levels of gravity; and plausibly valid
in its measure of severity.

We are certain that the procedures were carried out as planned.
The medical student worked under local supervision of the an-
thropologists and with the project physician's technical guidance.
Laboratory tests were conducted by competent specialists. The

* We are grateful to psychologist Francisco Franco Ibarra for his help in this
task.

physicians who analyzed data from the protocols, arrived at diagnoses, and scored the results followed the guidelines which had been prepared long before the clinical data were available. Finally, the statistical manipulations were carried out by competent personnel, and analysis of the results, completed by the project physician, was discussed at length with the anthropologists and submitted for criticism to several experienced clinicians.

5

Results

Indications of Social Stress

Asustados recognize that their condition can be more or less severe, and that when prolonged and severe it will end in death. Nevertheless, we did not assess levels of severity of susto. An earlier attempt to link symptom severity with severity of fright failed to disclose a relationship (O'Nell 1972:4–5).

The Social Stress Gauge produced ordinal measurements in which any one individual could be compared with any other to determine whether the first was higher, lower, or equal to the second. Because of the cumulative scoring procedures, we assumed that higher scores indicated higher levels of social stress.

Table 1 reports the test of the hypothesis that asustados would register higher social-stress scores than matched persons who, although sick, did not attribute any part of their problem to susto. We established as acceptable a probability level of 0.05 percent.

TABLE 1
SOCIAL STRESS SCORES:
ASUSTADOS AND CONTROLS

Culture	U	z	Probability Level
Chinantec	154.5	−1.22	>0.05†
Zapotec	33.5	—	≤0.025*
Mestizo	106.5	−1.75	≤0.04*

Mann–Whitney U Test

* Significant at ≤0.05, one tail.
† Not significant.

TABLE 2

SOCIAL STRESS SCORES:
ASUSTADOS AND CONTROLS

Gender	U	z	Probability Level
All Males	42.5	—	≤0.025*
All Females	537.0	−1.60	≤0.05*

Mann-Whitney U Test

* Significant at ≤0.05, one tail.

A positive association existed between high scores for stress and complaints of susto in all three communities. The association proved statistically significant for the Zapotec and Mestizo groups, but fell just short of the 0.05 level among the Chinantecs.

We then segregated males and females across the sample without respect to cultural affiliation, the results of which are shown in table 2. Again, a positive association occurred in the two tests, in each case statistically significant. Inferentially, regardless of culture, a high level of social stress and complaints of susto were associated among both men and women.

Tables 1 and 2 are somewhat redundant, but they require different data alignments so that the ordinal positions of the Social Stress Gauge are somewhat different. One could not assume that, given the results in table 1, those in table 2 would follow.

We employed one further test of the basic hypothesis by controlling cultural affiliation, gender, and age simultaneously. Since the results shown in tables 1 and 2 were in the direction predicted, but failed to attain statistical significance for the Chinantec sample, tests of the matched pairs were limited to community consideration rather than opened to a total sample analysis. The figures in table 3 show that, when matched by relative age, sex, and ethnic group, asustados registered significantly higher levels of stress than controls among Zapotecs and Mestizos, but the association fell just short of the acceptable level of significance among Chinantecs.

TABLE 3

SOCIAL STRESS:
MATCHED PAIRS

Culture	T	Probability Level
Chinantec	68	>0.05†
Zapotec	10	≤0.01*
Mestizo	19	≤0.005*

Wilcoxon Matched-Pairs Signed-Ranks Test

* Significant at ≤0.05, one tail.
† Not significant.

Indications of Psychiatric Impairment

The results (table 4) show no statistical differences between asustados and controls with respect to psychiatric impairments. The screening score failed to differentiate between asustada women and their controls or between the two male samples. To state this important finding somewhat differently, symptoms tapped by this screening instrument were not significantly different when persons actively complaining of susto were compared with those who were not. Susto is not associated with psychiatric impairment as measured by the 22-Item Screening Score.

TABLE 4

MODIFIED 22-ITEM SCREENING SCORE:
GENDER

Gender	U	z	Probability Level
All Males	63.5	−1.58	≥0.06†
All Females	658.0	−0.48	≥0.32†

Mann-Whitney U Test

† Not significant.

TABLE 5

MODIFIED 22-ITEM SCREENING SCORE:
CULTURE

Culture	U	z	Probability Level
Chinantec	155.0	−1.12	≥0.13†
Zapotec	62.5	−1.38	≥0.08†
Mestizo	140.0	−0.68	≥0.24†

Mann-Whitney U Test

† Not significant.

Are these results truly ". . . a rough indication of where people lie on a continuum of impairment in life functioning due to very common types of psychiatric symptoms" (Langner 1962:269), the purpose for which the index was adapted? Or were they simply chance results obtained by an instrument that may have been inadequate for tapping the cognitive world of these Mexican peasants? The following speaks to that issue. Although individuals' scores did range broadly up and down the scale, their distribution failed to differentiate those with susto from those without. This finding was as true of one community as of the others (table 5).

Moreover, failure to find a statistical association between having susto and a high score on the test for psychiatric impairment was characteristic of both men and women (table 4).

An interesting and provocative pattern did appear in that, when a break-even point was established at the 11.5 level, women, regardless of culture, consistently scored above that level, rather than below it. In contrast, men scored high *and* low with equal frequency in the Zapotec and Mestizo groups, whereas Chinantec males scored below that break-even point three times more frequently than they scored above it (table 6). This pattern acquires more significance when compared with results from other cultural groups. Roberts et al. (1973:19) summarized their study of American Blacks, as follows:

TABLE 6

MODIFIED 22-ITEM SCREENING SCORE:
GENDER DIFFERENCES

Gender	High (above 11.5)	Low (below 11.5)	
All Males	12 (43%)	16 (57%)	
All Females	48 (65%)	27 (35%)	
Totals	60 (58%)	43 (42%)	N = 103 (100%)

The finding for this sample that females have higher scores than males is corroborated by every study reported but one which has examined symptom scores in relation to sex. [Also] . . . sexual status overrides both socioeconomic status and age. (Cf. Crandell and Dohrenwend; Gaitz and Scott)

In none of the three communities did level of education affect psychiatric impairment score. Moreover, even taking into account income differences in the Mestizo group, we could not find an association between economic status and either total score or the manner in which an individual's score was distributed between the physiological and psychological subsets.

In view of the fact that measures of organic health were available on the same respondents for whom we had 22-Item test scores, it seemed reasonable to find some association between high score on organic problems and high score on those three of the 22 items said to reflect physiological orientation. However, when these physiological items were selected out, and their scores compared with measures of severity of organic disease, no association was discovered (table 7).

An effort to find some correlation between these same physiological items and measures of gravity of disease was unrewarding (table 8).

The conclusion to be drawn is that, in these Oaxaca societies, as in social groups in the United States, women are emotionally

TABLE 7

CORRELATION BETWEEN PHYSIOLOGICAL ITEMS/SEVERITY AVERAGES:
ASUSTADOS AND CONTROLS

Culture	Controls				Asustados			
	r_s	t	df	Probability Level	r_s	t	df	Probability Level
Chinantec	0.26	1.11	17	>0.20†	0.3	1.31	17	>0.20†
Zapotec	0.16	0.05	10	>0.20†	0.1	0.34	12	>0.20†
Mestizo	0.17	0.71	17	>0.20†	0.44	1.92	15	>0.05†

Spearman Rho Test
† Not significant.

TABLE 8

CORRELATIONS BETWEEN PHYSIOLOGICAL ITEMS/GRAVITY AVERAGES:
ASUSTADOS AND CONTROLS

Culture	Controls				Asustados			
	r_s	t	df	Probability Level	r_s	t	df	Probability Level
Chinantec	0.56	2.81	17	<0.02*	0.32	1.36	17	>0.10†
Zapotec	0.06	0.19	10	>0.20†	0.12	0.41	12	>0.20†
Mestizo	−0.19	−0.84	17	>0.20†	0.21	0.84	15	>0.20†

Spearman Rho Test

* Significant at ≤0.05 level.
† Not significant.

taxed far more heavily than their male counterparts (O'Nell and Selby).

Seiler (1973:259) criticized such findings, however, because:

> The items are not as representative of psychiatric symptoms for men as for women, *i.e.*, there are not items eliciting typical *masculine* symptoms: aggressiveness, overt hostility, or active antagonism . . . understandably women tend to score higher on the scale than men.

Her criticism is persuasive and may help to explain why this and other psychiatric screening instruments have so consistently produced similar results (Gove and Tudor 1973; Roberts et al. 1973:19, 22, 24. See also O'Nell and Selby 1968: tables 3 and 4; Seijas 1972:177).

Seiler's criticism is based on a presumption that, because in the United States males are socialized to be more aggressive, acting out, or comfortable with, an open display of hostility, they would achieve lower scores on tests that assume the results of those socialization processes as normative. Conversely, because women in the United States are *not* socialized towards such norms, they tend to score high on the same measure. However, by no means all societies socialize their males for the same normative behavior as characterizes their socialization in the United States.

In both the Zapotec and Chinantec communities, norms for males *as well as* for females strongly constrain overt displays of either aggression or hostility, although this is more true of women than men. The sine qua non of success is to live tranquilly with one's fellows. Sanctions against those who transgress so important a social norm are most severe (O'Nell 1969. See also J. Nash 1967; M. Nash 1960). The cultural differences that produce the socialization goals distinctive to these peasant communities (as opposed to those in the United States) diminish the general importance of Seiler's criticism with respect to this study; nonetheless, it should be borne in mind when reading the results shown in table 6.

Our results also indicated that the cultural differences between Mestizo, Chinantec, and Zapotec samples did not significantly affect the results. That conclusion conformed to results obtained from populations in the United States—outside of New York City (Roberts et al. 1973:22; Gaitz and Scott, cited in Roberts et al.:7). On the contrary, data from New York City suggested how ethnicity may influence the results of this impairment measure (Crandell and Dohrenwend 1967:1535; Haberman, cited in Roberts et al.:8). In sum, these data from Oaxaca's culturally diverse communities show no association between ethnicity and scores, whereas use of the test in the United States produced mixed results.

In summary, then, what do these results show? They offered a rough measure of real psychiatric symptoms within each of the gender samples and in each of the societies. They presented a suggestive pattern in which women scored higher than men in all three ethnic groups. Furthermore, when a median score of 11.5 points was established to differentiate those with high symptom scores from those with low, men of the respective groups never scored above that median more frequently than below it; contrastively, women never scored below the median more frequently than above it. These gender-specific results fell just short of statistical significance, but their directional tendency conformed, with a single exception, to the results obtained by all other applications of the screening score. Discovery that gender differences were not as pronounced in these results as in others highlights the significant influence of cultural value systems. In this case, the values strongly emphasized the importance of cooperative and nonaggressive behavior for individuals of both sexes, norms particularly powerful in the Indian groups.

Langner summarized his findings from samples in Tehuantepec and Mexico City, as follows:

> The existence of a genuine sex difference in symptoms is given credence when supported by findings from studies of several contrasting cultural groups and when such findings are consistent despite

the different techniques of gathering the information, different personnel, translation problems, the variation in meanings of symptoms, and the contrasting cultural modes of expressing mental disturbances. (1965:383)

Finally, taken individually, score by score, these results showed remarkable variability up and down the measuring scale among both men and women, but they did not distinguish asustado patients from others.

A positive correlation did occur between the social stress and 22-Item Screening measures (table 9). Some psychiatric impairment is related to high levels of social stress. This is commonsensical since we would expect a person scoring high on social stress to manifest higher levels of emotional difficulty. However, it does not follow that each instrument was measuring the same components. Rather, the 22-Item score assessed symptoms, and the Social Stress Gauge reported some psychological distress, which is inherent in a person acknowledging that he is not performing up to his own standards. Based on the results shown in table 4, we concede some overlap in what these instruments were measuring. We interpret this as "distress" in the social stress measure and as "dysfunction" in the psychiatric impairment measure.

The correlations were positive for both asustados and controls in the Mestizo community and for asustados only among the Chinantecs. They were not significant for either the experimental or the control group among Zapotecs, nor for the Chinantec controls.

Indications of Disease

The clinical findings are presented in three parts: the first is that of morbidity—that is, all disease manifestations encountered. The second refers to their impact on the patients; on the one hand, the extent to which they threaten their life (i.e., their

TABLE 9

SOCIAL STRESS/22-ITEM

Culture	Controls				Asustados			
	r_s	t	df	Probability Level	r_s	t	df	Probability Level
Chinantec	0.31	1.35	17	>0.10†	0.45	2.32	19	<0.05*
Zapotec	0.36	1.22	10	>0.20†	0.29	0.95	10	>0.20†
Mestizo	0.66	3.62	17	<0.01*	0.56	2.62	15	<0.02*

Spearman Rho Test

* Significant at ≦0.05 level.
† Not significant.

gravity) and on the other hand the extent to which they impede daily activities (i.e., their severity). The last section examines the association between these indications of disease and a patient's death. In each section, the goal is to discover differences between patients with susto and those without.

Disease indications encountered in patients were analyzed in four sections. In the first, signs and symptoms were analyzed to determine whether susto complaints were associated with one or several symptoms that would be indicative of disease processes to a physician. In the second section, we determined quantitatively whether asustados were characterized by a greater number of diagnosed conditions. In the third section, we made an effort to associate susto with one or several classes of disease classified by the World Health Organization. In the final section, we looked at the range of problems reported by laboratory tests of blood and stool.

Pain was the most frequently reported symptom among all patients, asustados as well as controls. Pain in the dorsolumbar region (back) occurred in almost one-half of the control patients (23 cases), and in a third of the asustados (17 cases). Among asustados, abdominal pain (17 cases) was more frequent than among the controls (10 cases). Pain of the lower extremities occurred in 16 asustados and in 13 controls. Muscular pains in general, regardless of location, were more problematic for the controls than for the asustados. None of these differences was statistically significant.

Anorexia (lack of appetite), in contrast, occurred in 12 asustados and in none of the controls. However, because lack of appetite so frequently recurs in so many sicknesses, statistical significance is not enough in itself to credit it as an indicator of susto. But a combination of this symptom with lack of motivation, asthenia, tiredness, and loss of weight represents an attack on one's general state of health and was found to be more frequent among asustados than among controls. This proved consistent whether comparing asustados with others in sex-specific populations or across ethnic groups. This cluster of symptoms—

lack of appetite, debility, tiredness, lack of motivation, and weight loss—occurred in 16 asustado patients and in only five of the others, a difference that is highly significant from a statistical point of view ($x^2 = 7.3$ df $= 1$ p<0.01). Apart from its statistical significance, this difference has important implications because we know that such an attack upon the body weakens the defenses of victims against other insults to the organism, such as infectious processes or complications. Apart from this symptom cluster, the remaining ones do not occur in sufficient number or variety to make possible a clear differentiation between the two groups. Nor do they point to one organ or system in which susto victims are more wont to localize their difficulties.

The diagnosticians reported 794 organic problems among the 100 patients. Of these, they agreed on 640, or 81 percent. Of those diagnoses on which they failed to coincide, 78 were made by one scorer, and 74 by the other. In sum, there was agreement on 81 percent of the diagnoses, with disagreement on 19 percent. Level of agreement seems not to have been affected by whether susto was or was not a constituent of a patient's condition.

Differences between diagnosticians did not affect the results: both reported more organic sickness among asustados. It would have been quite a different matter if one had reported more organic problems among the asustados with the other diagnosing more among the controls.

Each scorer reported more emotional difficulties among asustados than among other patients. However, the differences between those evaluations were quite dramatic. One reported a total of 16 patients suffering mental health problems, whereas the other found 34. They agreed on only 11 patients in whom both diagnosed pathology, and another 61 in whom neither encountered symptoms. They disagreed on the remaining 28 individuals. Statistically, their differences were significant and could not have occurred by chance ($x^2 = 13.7$ df $= 2$ p<0.05).

This difference becomes the more notable considering the diagnoses each physician assigned the same patients. Of the 11 cases on which they both reported that pathology was present, they coincided only once on the nature of the problem: nervous depression. In the remaining 10 evaluations, one physician was inclined to diagnose "psychosis," whereas the other leaned to "psychophysiological reaction of the central nervous system."

These gross discrepancies may be explained by several factors, of which one is the training provided physicians. Given the biological emphasis in contemporary medical education, it is hardly surprising that these two general-practice physicians should be in considerable disagreement. Difficulties in diagnosis are legion when the patient is of one culture or social class and the physician of another, but they are far more problematic when the difficulty is seated in the emotions (see Waxler 1974). For example, one scorer reported not one single emotional pathology among the 28 Mestizos, although he found pathology among 15 percent of the Zapotecs, and 37 percent of the Chinantecs. The other found 25 percent of the Mestizos to evidence pathology, 15 percent of the Zapotecs, and 61 percent of the Chinantecs. It appears that the greater the cultural chasm between physician and patient the more numerous the mental health problems reported. Were these individuals *really* mentally disturbed, or was the physician distracted by the manner in which they presented themselves—and their complaints—leading him to interpret these as evidence of aberration?

The diagnoses arrived at—organic as well as emotional— provided a patient's health portrait. This portrait comprised diagnoses of symptoms, syndromes, and diseases—in short, everything considered of significance by the diagnostic panel. One scorer arrived at an average of 4.46 diagnoses for each asustado, but only 3.82 for each control patient. The other recorded 4.72 and 3.88, respectively. That is, each independently found more sickness among the asustados. Combining their diagnoses and eliminating repetitions, asustados averaged 5.6, contrasting with 4.7 for each control. Among the 50 susto cases, 280 conditions were reported, in contrast to 235 among the others. This difference could occur by chance in less than 5 percent of cases ($x^2 = 3.93$ df 1 = 1 $p<0.05$).

One of the scoring physicians reported an average of 4.14 organic problems for each asustado, and 3.82 for each control. The other found 4.24 and 3.68, respectively. That is, both of these diagnosticians reported more organic health problems among the asustados, although their findings failed to reach the accepted level of significance. Even when their diagnoses were combined, and repetition eliminated, their diagnoses failed to differentiate between these groups at an acceptable level of significance.

One physician-scorer reported psychoemotional problems in 16 asustado cases, but in none of the controls. The other found problems among 24 of the former, and among 10 of the latter. In each instance, these differences were statistically significant. Another means of processing these data was to combine the scorers' diagnoses. To do this, we considered as pathologic *only* those for whom both scorers reported a problem. Those scored as free of problems were those for whom neither physician reported a diagnosis, and "possibly sick" were those for whom only one of the diagnosticians reported a problem. According to this procedure, 11 asustados were diagnosed with problems, 18 possibly sick (5 according to one scorer, 13 according to the other), and 21 without problems. That same procedure found no pathology among the controls, although 10 were possibly sick, and 40 completely without problems. These results differentiated one group from the other at highly significant levels ($x^2 = 19.18$ df $= 2$ p<0.01). Obviously, these findings of emotional disturbance affected the total morbidity results in such a way that asustados were characterized by a total of far more diagnosed problems than were controls. Although psychoemotional problems tipped the balance, they should not distract attention from the other finding that organic health problems were also more numerous among the asustado population, although they failed to arrive at our level of statistical significance.

Analysis of the quantitative dimensions of morbidity indicated that psychoemotional difficulties represented only 6.1 percent of total pathology among asustados, with 93.9 percent represented by organic difficulties. Those differences were even larger among the controls, 2.4 percent and 97.6 percent, respectively. Did these differences accurately reflect the relative importance of each of these kinds of problems for these individuals? To estimate their relative importance more definitively, one must take other matters into consideration.

In the present state of sophistication of medical training, a nonspecialist is capable of diagnosing different kinds of organic pathology, but only rarely possesses that competence when presented with emotional problems. Furthermore, the clinician is provided several procedures by which to diagnose conclusively many organic conditions, but this is less true with psychoemotional difficulties.

Another problem suggested by these results is how to define the boundary between organic and emotional problems. A patient suffering headaches, with hypertension, who appears in an anxious state, may be diagnosed as follows: hypertension, migraine, and anxiety neurosis. This diagnosis includes two organic problems and one of an emotional nature. However, another clinician might justifiably diagnose an anxiety neurosis, with hypertension, resulting in migraine headaches as one mental health problem with organic repercussions. Which of the two would be considered the more correct?

The present state of general practice contributes to clinical work-ups being oriented towards discovery of organic problems, and residual difficulties being attributed to psychoemotional causes. Our research offered little opportunity for development of a meaningful relationship between the examining physician and his patients, much less a chance to follow up a diagnosis. In addition, the examining clinician was trained as a generalist, and diagnoses were developed by a panel of physicians with traditional clinical preparation. It therefore came as no surprise to find the results so heavily weighted in favor of organic problems.

Although it has proved methodologically useful to separate

Carole Browner

Chinantec dividing harvest of maize cultivated by her husband and his brother. Maize was planted on their mother's private lands.

John Krej

Mestiza preparing tortillas.

Young Chinantec receiving counsel from ritual elder on assuming public office—*cargo*.

Fatigued Mestizo resting before being cured for susto.

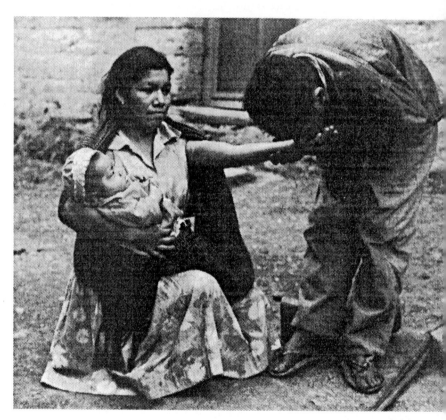

Chinantec asustada undergoing treatment.

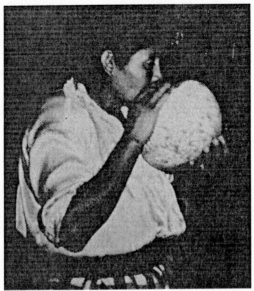

Zapotec susto specialist calls victim's name into a gourd to induce return of her vital essence. The greater the distance that separates her vital essence from her body, the more often her name is called into the gourd.

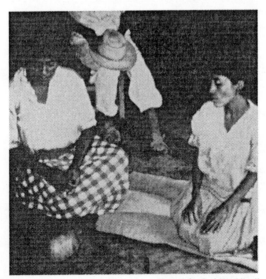

Zapotec specialist and susto patient wait for a diagnosis to be revealed by eggs covered by gourd.

Zapotec susto patient holding palms out to be sprayed by ritual healer.

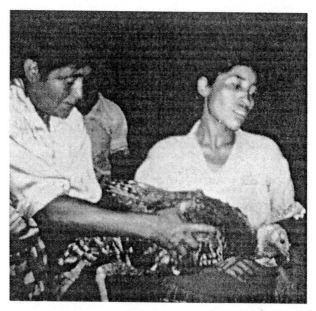

Zapotec specialist "passes" a sacrificial turkey over her patient's body. The bird's severed head is then offered to propitiate the spirit captor of the asustada's vital essence.

Zapotec asustada and her female "supplicant" at the embankment where the susto occurred. A female and a male "supplicant" are commonly selected to attend final healing rites to strengthen the summons to her vital essence.

Zapotec susto specialist chewing herbs. She will apply the paste of herbs and spittle to the arms of her patient to strengthen her body.

Strengthening the body of a Zapotec asustada by application of herbal paste.

organic problems from those of an emotional nature, from the conceptual point of view we found it best to consider the patient as a whole person responding in diverse ways to stressors.

Classes of Diseases

Diseases encountered in these patients were classified according to the *International Classification of Diseases,* 8th revised edition, World Health Organization. Of the 17 major classifications of diseases, 15 were found among our diagnoses (table 10).

There were no diseases in ICD Group XI, "pregnancy, childbirth and postpartum complications," nor in Group XV, "certain causes of perinatal morbidity and mortality," so these groups were not included in the table. The lack of diagnoses in the first was due to the fact that pregnancy is perceived as a normal condition among the rural population, and rarely do they seek consultation for problems attributed to pregnancy. We attended neither normal nor difficult births during the study. With regard to the second group, we have already indicated that the study included only persons 18 years and older, which excluded the recently born to which Group XV alludes.

In this table we include a summary of the pathologies encountered in the 100 patients examined, a report of differences between asustados and controls, and the distribution of diseases.

The entities most frequently diagnosed were those from Group I, Infective and Parasitic Diseases, which totaled 110 among the 100 patients. There were more diagnoses than patients because in populations like these it often happens that a person suffers from more than one infectious and/or parasitic disease at the same time. This is also illustrated by the group of diseases that came second in order of frequency: Diseases of Blood and Blood-Forming Organs (Group IV). This group also includes "Unspecified anemia," suggesting nutritional deficiencies and/or chronic blood loss due either to parasite infestation or to recurring infections. Eighty-five instances of anemia were diagnosed,

TABLE 10
DIAGNOSED DISEASES IN 50 PATIENTS WITH SUSTO AND 50 WITHOUT SUSTO

Disease Classes*	ICD Key	Chinantecs **Asu.	Con.	Zapotecs Asu.	Con.	Mestizos Asu.	Con.	Total Asu.	Con.
I Infective & Parasitic Diseases	006–136	33	23	14	11	14	15	61	49
Amoeba	006	5	5	9	9	10	8	24	22
Tuberculosis	011	1	0	3	2	1	0	5	2
Onchocerciasis	125.3	8	2	0	0	0	0	8	2
Ascariasis	127	7	5	0	0	0	0	7	5
Intestinal Parasitosis without specification	129	7	8	1	0	3	7	11	15
Other Infective & Parasitic Diseases		5	3	1	0	0	0	6	3
II Neoplasms	140–239	1	2	3	0	0	0	4	2
III Endocrine, Nutritional & Metabolic Diseases	240–279	1	1	2	0	1	1	4	2
IV Diseases of Blood & Blood-Forming Organs									
Unspecified anemia	285.9	17	15	13	6	16	18	46	39
V Mental Disorders	290–315	27	9	6	0	4	1	37	10
Psychoses	299	6	3	3	0	1	1	10	4

TABLE 10 (continued)

Neurosis	300	5	0	1	0	0	0	6	0
Depressive neurosis	300.4	1	0	0	0	2	0	3	0
Personality disorders	301.9	0	0	1	0	1	0	2	0
Symptoms not elsewhere classified	306	13	0	1	0	0	0	14	0
Sleep disorders	306.4	2	6	0	0	0	0	2	6
VI Diseases of the Nervous System & Sense Organs	320–389	7	7	10	7	14	4	31	18
Hereditary & Familial Diseases of Nervous System	345.9	2	2	0	0	1	0	3	2
Conjunctivitis & Ophthalmia	360	3	4	0	2	0	0	3	6
Refractive defects	370	1	1	0	0	2	0	3	1
Pterygium	372	0	0	5	2	8	2	13	4
Cataract	374	0	0	2	1	1	0	3	1
Blindness in one eye	379.3	0	0	1	0	0	1	1	1
Diseases in the ear & mastoid process	389.9	1	0	1	0	0	0	2	0
Others		0	0	1	2	2	1	3	3
VII Diseases of the Circulatory System	390–458	14	10	6	4	1	8	21	22
Diseases of the endocardium	397	0	1	1	0	0	0	1	1

TABLE 10 (*continued*)

Disease Classes*	ICD Key	Chinantecs **Asu.	Con.	Zapotecs Asu.	Con.	Mestizos Asu.	Con.	Total Asu.	Con.
Essential hypertension (benign)	401	7	4	1	1	0	4	8	9
Poorly defined symptoms of the heart	429	1	0	0	1	0	1	1	2
Varicose veins	454.9	0	4	1	1	0	1	1	6
Hypotension	458.0	5	1	0	0	0	0	5	1
Others		1	0	3	1	1	2	5	3
VIII Diseases of the Respiratory System	460–519	6	14	3	0	9	8	18	22
Diseases of the pharynx & tonsils	462,463	4	5	0	0	0	1	4	6
Chronic bronchitis	491	0	1	0	0	2	1	2	2
Tonsilar Hypertrofy	500	0	2	0	0	2	2	2	4
Deviated Septum	504	0	5	2	0	1	0	3	5
Nasal Polyp	505	0	0	0	0	2	1	2	1
Other diseases of upper respiratory tract	508	2	0	1	0	1	2	4	2
Others		0	1	0	0	1	1	1	2

TABLE 10 (*continued*)

IX Diseases of the Digestive System	520–577	17	8	10	3	10	10	37	21
Dental caries	521.0	7	4	3	1	6	6	16	11
Missing teeth (acquired)	525.0	5	1	1	1	4	1	10	3
Gastritis & Duodenitis	535	1	1	7	0	0	1	8	2
Chronic enteritis	563.9	3	2	0	0	0	0	3	2
Others		1	0	4	1	0	2	5	3
X Diseases of Genito–Urinary System	580–629	2	5	1	1	2	3	5	9
Nephritis	583	0	0	1	0	1	0	2	0
Diseases of breast, ovary, fallopian tubes, parametrium	614	0	1	0	0	0	1	0	2
Leukorrhea	629.3	0	2	0	0	0	1	0	3
Others		2	2	0	1	1	1	3	4
XII Diseases of the Skin & Subcutaneous Tissues	680–709	0	1	0	0	2	1	2	2
XIII Diseases of the Musculo-skeletal System & Connective Tissue	710–738	2	8	1	7	4	13	7	28
Arthritis & rheumatism, except rheumatic fever	712	2	4	0	6	4	7	6	17

TABLE 10 (continued)

Disease Classes*	ICD Key	Chinantecs **Asu.	Con.	Zapotecs Asu.	Con.	Mestizos Asu.	Con.	Total Asu.	Con.
Osteomyelitis & other diseases of bone & joint	713.0–717.9	0	3	1	1	0	3	1	7
Diseases of spinal discs	725.1	0	1	0	0	0	1	0	2
Other diseases of musculo-skeletal system	728.7–728.9	0	0	0	0	0	2	0	2
XIV Congenital Anomalies	745.0	0	0	0	1	0	0	0	1
XVI Symptoms & Ill-Defined Conditions	780–796	0	1	7	3	0	4	7	8
Edema & Hydropsy	782.6	0	0	1	0	0	2	1	2
Hypertrophic lymph nodes	782.7	0	0	2	0	0	1	2	1
Enlarged liver	785.1	0	0	2	0	0	0	2	0
Others		0	1	2	3	0	1	2	5
XVII Accidents, Poisonings, & Violence (Nature of Injury)	N800–N922	0	1	0	0	0	1	0	2
Total Diagnoses		127	105	76	43	77	87	280	235
Number of persons examined		19	19	14	12	17	19	50	50

* Based on the *International Classification of Diseases* (Clasificación Internacional de Enfermedades), 8th Edition, Organización Panamericana de la Salud, Washington, D.C., 1967.
** Asu = Asustados, Con = Controls

a very elevated percentage. There were 58 cases from Group IX, Diseases of the Digestive System, occupying third place in frequency of pathology. The largest number of these—27 cases— was dental caries. Next were Diseases of the Nervous System and Sense Organs (Group VI, inflated by a relatively minor problem, pterygium (fleshiness of the ocular conjunctiva), of which there were 17 among the 49 cases in the group. Mental Disorders (Group V) occupied fifth place in frequency with 47 cases, 14 of which were diagnosed as a psychosis. It is most unlikely that this diagnosis indicated a loss of contact with reality; it was more likely a judgment that one of the diagnosing scorers made for divers neurotic and psychoneurotic disorders. After these five groups of diseases, there followed diseases of the circulatory system (43 cases) and those of the respiratory system (40 cases); of the osteomuscular system and conjunctiva tissue, there were 35 cases; and so on until problems of low prevalence were reached, such as accidents, poisoning, violent acts, and congenital anomalies.

In all, 515 diseases were diagnosed in 100 patients; an average of 5.15 diagnosed diseases per patient.

Diseases that better differentiated asustados and controls were those from Group V, Mental Disorders. They were diagnosed in 58 percent of the asustado patients and in 20 percent of the controls, a statistically significant difference. Differences also occurred at the society level; among Chinantecs this diagnosis was made in 95 percent of the asustado patients and in 47 percent of the controls. Among Zapotecs, mental disease was diagnosed in 36 percent of the asustados and in none of the controls; and, among Mestizos, in 35 percent of the asustados and in only 5 percent of the controls. We do not know for certain why differences so marked occurred between one society and another; it may have reflected reality or, more likely, it indicated that the greater the cultural difference between doctor and patient, the greater the probability of classifying as mental pathology thought patterns that are culturally acceptable to the patient but symptomatic to the clinician. It represents an interesting methodological problem to be addressed by both medical and anthropological research. For whatever the reason, the difference between asustados and controls was consistent and confirmed what has already been noted in the quantitative pathology section.

With regard to the emotional pathology encountered, the most frequent diagnosis among asustados was "symptoms not elsewhere classified" (14 cases). Subsumed under that classification was the diagnosis of "psychophysiological reaction of the central nervous system." Only one of our two scorers arrived at that diagnosis. Obviously, it was a diagnosis communicating little information as to the type of pathology a patient had. It was a clinical judgment that some pathology was present; however, in the absence of sufficient data, it remained impossible to make a more precise diagnosis. The second most frequent diagnosis under Mental Disorders (Group V) was psychosis; this was arrived at by one of the diagnosticians in 10 cases: 6 Chinantecs, 3 Zapotecs, and 1 Mestizo. Review of the protocols by the project physician showed insufficient data for diagnosing so serious a condition, defined as "a loss of contact with reality"; hence, we interpreted this to mean that in the diagnostician's judgment there was mental pathology, but he lacked the data (or knowledge) to arrive at a more precise diagnosis. In 6 of the asustados, neurosis was found; in 3, depressive neurosis; in 2, personality disorders; and 2, sleep disorders. In all, 37 diagnoses of mental pathology were made in 29 asustado patients. In contrast, among the controls, 10 diagnoses were made for 10 patients; of these, 6 were sleep disorders and 4 were psychoses. The contrast between the relative proliferation of mental pathology among asustado patients and its scarcity among controls was evident. Independent of the competence of the physician-scorers to perform diagnoses with certainty—whether because of their clinical training or experience, or because of the level of clinical information on which they depended—the fact is that each independently reported more diagnoses of psychoemotional and psychiatric pathology among asustados.

Diseases listed in Group II (Neoplasms) as "tumors without specifying malignity" affected 4 asustados and 2 controls, and the same occurred with diseases in Group III, Endocrine, Nutritional, and Metabolic Diseases, with 4 asustados and 2 controls affected.

Following mental disorders, the diseases that most clearly differentiated asustados from controls were those from Group IX, Diseases of the Digestive System, for which there were 37 diagnoses among asustados and 21 among controls (that is, for each such condition among the controls there were 1.76 among the asustados. This difference was statistically significant ($x^2 =$ 9.4 df $= 1$ p$<$0.01). The most frequent diagnosis within this group was diseases of the teeth: 16 instances of dental caries among asustados against 11 among controls; missing teeth in 10 asustados and in 3 controls. In addition, 6 cases of gastritis and duodenitis among asustados against 4 among controls. For "other" diseases of this system, 5 were identified among asustados and 3 among controls.

Diseases in Group VI, Diseases of the Nervous System and Sense Organs, were also significantly higher among asustados—31 cases—in contrast to the controls with 18 cases. This difference was also statistically significant ($x^2 = 6.7$ df $= 1$ p$<$0.01). Within this disease group, the most frequent problem of the asustados was pterygium (fleshiness of the ocular conjunctiva), which affected 13 patients, of which only 4 were controls. More serious eye ailments than pterygium were refractive defects (3 asustados and 1 control), conjunctivitis and ophthalmia (3 asustados and 6 controls), cataract (3 asustados and 1 control), and blindness in one eye (1 asustado and 1 control). In all, 23 asustados and 13 controls had eye diseases. Group VI also revealed 3 cases of epilepsy among asustados, 2 among controls; 2 cases of partial loss of hearing among asustados and none among controls; and 3 diagnoses from each group were classified as "other" diseases.

We have seen that in three groupings of the International

Classification, Mental Disorders, Diseases of the Digestive System, and Diseases of the Nervous System and Sense Organs, pathology was more elevated among the asustado patients. In contrast, the diseases in Group I, Infectious and Parasitic Diseases, were not distinguishable between the two samples. Only one, onchocerciasis, proved more characteristic of the asustados. Taken as a whole, of this group of diseases, 61 were found among 50 asustado patients (1.22 for each patient) and 49 among controls (0.98 for each patient). This difference was greatest among Chinantecs, among whom there were 1.7 of these diseases for each asustado patient and 1.2 for each control patient. A high prevalence of morbidity from environmental causes evidently exists in this municipio. In the other two ethnic groups, problems were consistently more numerous among asustados than among controls, although of a less severe nature. The majority of these problems were intestinal parasites. Among the asustados, 42 of 61 of these cases were parasites (24 amoebiosis, 7 ascariasis, and 11 "others"); among controls, 42 of 49 cases were parasites (22 amoebiosis, 5 ascariasis, and 15 "others"). Besides intestinal parasites, 5 cases of pulmonary tuberculosis were diagnosed among asustados and 2 among controls; 8 cases of onchocerciasis were diagnosed among asustados and 2 among controls; and 6 cases of "other" diseases were found in this group among asustados and 3 among controls. With the exception of "other" intestinal parasites present in 11 asustados and 15 controls, there were more diagnoses among asustados in each of the diseases of this group.

With respect to onchocerciasis, 8 cases were found among asustados, and only 2 among controls, a statistically significant difference ($x^2 = 4$ df $= 1$ p<0.05).

Diseases that did not distinguish between asustados and controls were those of the circulatory system (21 asustados and 22 controls), those of the respiratory system (18 asustados and 22 controls), those of the genitourinary system (5 asustados and 9 controls), those of the skin and subcutaneous cellular tissue (2 asustados and 2 controls) and "poorly defined symptoms and illness states" (7 asustados and 8 controls).

Of the 17 major classifications, Group XIII diseases (those of the musculoskeletal system and connective tissue), were diagnosed significantly fewer times among asustados than among controls. This proved to be a unique finding. In this group, 28 controls and only 7 asustados were diagnosed with osteomuscular problems, a difference that was statistically significant ($x^2 = 19$ df $= 1$ p<0.01). Within this group, the more frequent diagnoses were of rheumatoid arthritis and related pathological conditions (17 among controls and 6 among asustados), with an important statistical difference ($x^2 = 6.8$ df $= 1$ p<0.01) for one subgroup, "unspecified osteo-arthritis and myalgias" (7 controls and 1 asustado), "pathology of spinal discs" (2 controls and no asustados) and other ailments of this class (2 controls and no asustados). It is hoped that later studies will provide explanation of these differences.

Analysis of qualitative morbidity found that asustados and controls were differently affected by diseases endemic to their environs. A number of the symptoms and signs presented, although found diffused in many disease entities (e.g., loss of appetite, loss of weight, debility, lack of motivation), are noteworthy in that they indicate a general state of debilitation, organic as well as emotional. Digestive diseases and anemia are conditions compatible with severe malnutrition, often with fatal consequences. Can it be concluded that susto is the equivalent of malnutrition? The answer is "no." By no means is each asustado patient suffering notable malnutrition. Indeed, there are asustados without any evidence of malnutrition! In the same way, and in spite of the statistical results, it cannot be said that susto is equivalent to onchocerciasis, or that susto and dental caries are labels for the same problem. Nor can it be argued that susto equals pterygium, or that it represents other diseases of the digestive system, or that asustados are mentally ill. Just because those diseases were sometimes associated with susto, the cause of a susto complaint cannot be attributed exclusively to any of them. Whatever its origin, in patients with susto there is more involvement of organic or emotional problems, or both; that is, the susto problem should not be assessed either in a fragmentary fashion or as a problem without relevance to cosmopolitan medicine.

What, then, may be the common denominator of dental caries, pterygium, diseases of the digestive system, of the nervous system and sense organs, onchocerciasis, and anemia? Medical texts produce no agent or mechanism capable of producing so diverse a group of pathologies. Instead, the organic pathology we uncovered is widely distributed among these populations. Asustados shared with others in the burden of disease, but not equally. Among Chinantecs, onchocerciasis was endemic, but asustados were more susceptible; pterygium was endemic to these peasants, but it affected the asustados more often; anemia was very prevalent, but occurred even more often among asustados and, when life's hardships generated emotional problems, asustados were even more likely to suffer. In sum, if a population as a whole requires medical attention, it will be found that asustados within that population are more in need.

Results of Laboratory Tests

Laboratory findings were the most objective of our assessments of health status because the technicians examined only evidence produced by the body. We measured hemoglobin and hematocrit levels to assess levels of anemia. Hemoglobin, the principal component of red blood cells, is a protein which, combined with iron, functions to transport oxygen from the lungs to the tissues. Hematocrit represents the volume of red blood cells expressed as a percentage of the total blood. When hematocrit and/or hemoglobin decreases, transportation of oxygen to the tissues becomes deficient, and the person is said to suffer from anemia. There are many kinds of anemia, but in this instance we refer to anemia in general; its most probable cause is deficient ingestion or utilization of iron from food—nutritional anemia—owing to nutritional disorders, or the iron loss through

intestinal parasites, or hemorrhagenic disorders such as metror-
rhagia, dysenteries, and others. Anemia is not a disease in itself,
rather it signals an underlying pathology resulting from diverse
causes and helps to exacerbate other processes because it decreases tissue oxygenation.

Moreover, anemia is commonly made responsible for other
blood deficiencies, especially immunal processes. Additionally,
blood contains, as well as provides, components necessary to
homeostasis of the organism. For all these reasons, anemia is an
important indicator of a general state of poor health.

The normal level of hemoglobin in men, following the guidelines used by our laboratory, was 15.5 grams for each 100 milliliters of blood. Among asustado patients, levels averaged 12.47,
and among controls, 13.92; that is, although both groups were
below normal, asustado men had one-and-a-half grams less
hemoglobin than did controls. This difference—2.6 grams—was
largest among Chinantecs; in that community, asustado men had
12.12, with controls averaging 14.72. In the other two communities, male asustados continued to show lower levels of
hemoglobin than did controls, but the differences did not reach
levels of significance. Hematocrit levels showed the same tendency; male asustados consistently were in worse condition than
their counterpart controls, but these differences failed to attain
statistically significant levels.

The technical guidelines listed women's norms at 14.8 grams
of hemoglobin per 100 milliliters of blood, and between 35 and
48 percent of hematocrit. Women with susto scored an average
of 11.43 grams of hemoglobin, with controls scoring at 11.85.
In all three communities, asustadas had less hemoglobin than
did the others.

With respect to hematocrit levels, asustadas averaged 35.54
percent and controls 35.88 percent, a miniscule difference in
favor of controls. Save for this exception, the findings supported
what was found among males; that is, asustada patients tended
to be somewhat more anemic than control patients.

Parasitism in our patients can be assumed to be greater than that indicated since transport conditions made it impossible for us to examine more than a single stool sample per patient.

Of the 100 patients examined, one or more kinds of parasites were found in 74; the total number of diagnoses of parasitism was 101. Numerically, there were more diagnoses than patients due to polyparasitism in several individuals. This gives some idea of the ecological setting to which these patients must accommodate.

In sum, 80 percent of the asustado patients had one or more kinds of parasites and 68 percent of the controls were infested, a difference not statistically significant but which repeated itself in two ethnic groups and across both sexes. Among Zapotecs, 78 percent of the asustado patients had parasites, and 67 percent of the controls; among Mestizos, 81 percent of the asustados and 37 percent of the controls. In contrast, all Chinantec controls had parasite loads but *only* 90 percent of the asustados. With respect to gender, women in general hosted more parasites than men, 78 percent and 68 percent, respectively. In the total male sample, 79 percent of the asustados and 57 percent of the controls had parasite loads; among women, 81 percent of the asustadas and 72 percent of the controls had parasites.

Gravity and Severity

As was indicated earlier, levels of gravity and severity were evaluated for each patient by instruments specifically constructed for this investigation. These instruments were a "gravimeter" and a "severimeter," respectively. The two physicians who were to score them worked independently of one another, following a set of instructions prepared beforehand. The instruments, and instructions for their use, will be found in the Appendix:160.

To measure levels of gravity and severity, a four-component clinical protocol was developed. As earlier indicated, the four sections included a history of the disease and its development, symptoms reported by the patient together with his or her family background, findings from the physical examination, and results of the laboratory tests. Following the instructions, a scorer carefully calculated the gravity indicated by each component; later, he summed the scores of the four components, arriving at a total gravity score. The maximum possible gravity score was 40 points; a score of 40 indicated the imminence of death. Then, following similar procedures, the physician-scorers arrived at severity levels; again the maximum was 40 points, a total that suggested the patient was totally incapacitated.

The gravity and severity measures permitted the intervention of clinical judgments (unlike the thermometer, the reading of which does *not* introduce subjective factors). That created a doubt: could the subjectivity of our scorers have skewed the results to such an extent that the scores more accurately reflected their clinical judgments than the differences between patients?

An analysis of the scores provided each patient by the respective physician-evaluators showed that agreement between their judgments was very satisfactory, attaining a high level of significance, which speaks in favor of the reliability of the methods employed (table 11).

The sum of the four components of the protocol indicated each patient's total gravity. The minimum gravity found was 1 point and the maximum was 26, which showed a remarkable variability. The average gravity among men was 6 points, but somewhat higher, at 6.42, among women. This points out the

TABLE 11
AGREEMENT BETWEEN PHYSICIANS' EVALUATIONS

Culture	Severity Scores		Gravity Scores	
	r_s	Probability Level	r_s	Probability Level
Chinantec	0.77	$<0.001^*$	0.72	$<0.001^*$
Zapotec	0.90	$<0.01^*$	0.69	$<0.01^*$
Mestizo	0.68	$<0.001^*$	0.56	$<0.001^*$

Spearman Rho Test

* Significant at ≤ 0.05 level.

predominance of quite low levels of gravity, something to be expected in a group of ambulatory patients.

Male asustados scored an average of 7.42 points of gravity; controls scored 4.58. This difference is statistically significant (Mann-Whitney $U = 5.8$ $z = -1.838$ $p<0.05$). In comparing groups within each community, significant differences were discovered only among Zapotecs; nonetheless, in all communities, asustados consistently scored higher on gravity than their counterpart controls. Among Chinantecs, the average gravity of asustados was 8.93 and that of controls 5.72; among Zapotecs, it was 6.90 and 3.96, respectively; among Mestizos, 6.60 and 4.53, respectively.

Among women, findings were similar: the difference was statistically significant in comparing Zapotec asustadas and controls, and in comparing the total group of asustados and controls (Mann-Whitney $U = 489.5$ $z = -1.785$ $p<0.05$). The groups averaged: 7.01 for asustados and 5.84 for controls; for Chinantec women, it was 8.19 and 7.48, respectively; for Zapotec women, 8.12 and 5.05; and Mestizo women scored 5.18 and 4.55, respectively.

Not a single instance was observed, among either men or women, in which a group of controls equalled or surpassed gravity levels of the asustados! (See table 12.) The gravity levels of the latter were always greater; among Zapotecs, as well as among the total group of patients, it was significantly higher (reaching a statistical level of 0.05) than that of the controls. This consistency in the results indicated a clear association between suffering susto and presenting signs and symptoms of truly life-threatening disease.

A physician caring for a patient with susto should, consequently, assume his charge to be at greater risk of dying than another patient with similar characteristics, although without susto.

The level of gravity in asustado patients, according to the history of the disease, tended to be higher than that in controls, but the variations failed to reach statistical significance in any of

TABLE 12

ORGANIC ILLNESS SCORES:
ASUSTADOS AND CONTROLS
(COMPONENT TOTALS)

Community & Gender	U	Severity Probability Level	U	Gravity Probability Level
Chinantec	150.5	>0.05†	155.5	>0.05†
Zapotec	19.0	<0.001*	31.0	<0.01*
Mestizo	152.5	>0.05†	116.0	>0.05†
All Male	53.0	<0.02*	58.0	<0.05*
All Female	637.0	>0.05†	489.5	<0.05*

Mann-Whitney U Test

* Statistically significant at ≤0.05 level.
† Not significant.

the three communities. This may have been due to the scarcity of data collected on the clinical protocol. It is possible that a more detailed history would have permitted more precise measures of gravity, productive of greater differences between asustados and controls.

Measurement of patients' symptoms also produced higher gravity scores among asustados, but again without reaching the established level of significance. The same was true with respect to diseases that follow families through time.

The gravity level inferred from the physical examination was significantly higher among Zapotec asustados than among controls. In the other two groups, gravity among asustados was higher but failed to reach statistical significance. This was an important finding, inasmuch as what a clinician discovers during examination is generally more objective than what the patient reports (as indicated in the history) or what the patient reports in the way of symptoms. Extending this finding, it could be said that a careful physical examination should reveal an asustado to be more gravely sick than a patient without susto.

Laboratory tests were the most objective component of the

clinical protocol, in the sense that neither the examiner's nor the patient's judgment was involved. Evidence of anemia and intestinal parasitism showed significantly higher levels among Zapotec and Mestizo asustados than were shown in their respective controls. This finding was the most solid confirmation that asustados were more gravely afflicted than controls. Gravity here refers to a specific domain in which clinicians boast considerable authority. It does not measure psychoemotional problems, regardless of whether or not they are present in such a patient. Organically, a patient's condition is more life-threatening when he has susto than when he has not. Clearly this is a cause for concern on the part of attending physicians.

Disease limits activity in a distinct way in each case according to the disease and the way in which an individual responds. How can researchers measure the extent to which a disease limits customary activity? And how can we measure the percentage of customary activity a patient carries out despite being sick? *Severity* is an inference of the extent to which a disease impedes a person from carrying out customary activities. On our "severimeter," the maximum possible score was 40 points, a level implying total incapacitation. If a patient had 10 points of severity, we considered that his daily activity was reduced by 25 percent; that is, he was carrying out 75 percent of his customary activities.

The average level of severity among the 100 patients was 16.7. This represented 42 percent of 40 possible points, implying that this group of persons could carry out 58 percent of its daily activities. Men averaged 15.53, and women slightly more, or 17.16. The lowest severity was 5 points and the maximum 24.75, illustrating the variability in levels of pathology and/or in the responses of the examined patients.

With the exception of Chinantec women, asustados were more severely affected than controls in all groups. These differences reached statistical significance when we compared the male asustados with their controls, and when we compared all Zapotec susto cases with their controls. The association found between higher levels of severity and susto complaints among men was consistent with what has already been suggested. When a man finally acknowledges suffering susto, his problem has already seriously impeded his usual activities.

The severity index showed that the impact of susto on a patient's daily activities varied from one group to another. Among Chinantecs, its impact was minimal, and intermediate among Mestizos. It was strongest among Zapotecs, and more so among Zapotec men than women. These men averaged 13.6 points of severity when sick without susto, and 19.9 when their complaint included it. Women registered, respectively, 16.3 and 23 points. Susto raised the level of severity some 46 percent among Zapotec men and 41 percent among the women!

Why do the Zapotecs respond to disease with higher levels of severity than the Chinantecs when the latter are more gravely diseased? Cultural as well as biological factors may be involved.

The Spearman Rho Test was applied to discover whether severity increased as gravity scores went up. It was applied separately to the scores of both asustados and control groups. Among the latter, no significant correlation was found; that is, in an important number of controls, impairment did not correspond to the extent to which their lives were threatened. There were gravely sick patients with low severity scores, and vice versa. On the contrary, among the asustados, we found a statistically significant correlation between the extent to which their lives were threatened and the curtailment of their daily activities (table 13). That is, asustados showed greater homogeneity of response to disease. If the disease produced a low level of gravity, behavior was congruent and the patient was not severely incapacitated. However, when the conditions of these patients were adjudged to be life-threatening, the severity score was also high and a dramatic curtailment of activity was presumed. This positive correlation between gravity and severity confirmed that susto is a condition that truly affects an individual holistically. If asustado

TABLE 13
CORRELATION BETWEEN SEVERITY AND GRAVITY OF ILLNESS

Culture	r_s	Controls Probability Level	r_s	Asustados Probability Level
Chinantec	0.4	0.05<p<0.10†	0.9	≤0.001*
Zapotec	0.6	0.05<p<0.10†	0.9	≤0.001*
Mestizo	0.4	0.05<p<0.10†	0.5	≤0.05*

Spearman Rho Test
* Statistically significant at ≤0.05.
† Not significant.

patients were simply malingering, a high level of severity would have been expected, with a low level of gravity. Conversely, if susto was affecting an individual in a specific area, with a localized cancer, for example, a high gravity score would have been expected with low scores on severity. In clinical medicine, general exhaustion in a patient with susto should, consequently, cause alarm and alert attending staff to a life-threatening crisis.

Fatal Consequences

Important issues appeared in the analysis of deaths among patients with and without susto. First of all, was the case fatality rate greater among asustados? Second, what, in fact, did asustados die from? Third, were patients with higher gravity and severity scores more likely to succumb than those with lower scores?

The data on which the following analysis is based were collected seven years after completion of the field study. Information was obtained in the Zapotec and Mestizo communities by interviewing municipal authorities and inhabitants. The interviewer had a list of the original patients from each town, but he did not know which among them had suffered susto. He inquired about the state of health of each person and took down

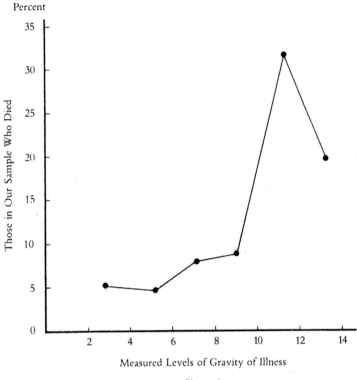

Figure 1

the names of those who had died and the official cause of death. In the Chinantec community, this information was collected by a local resident.

Over the seven-year period, eight asustado patients had died but none of their matched controls. The seven-year loss among asustados was 17 percent (8 deaths among 47 patients followed up); there were no deaths among the 48 control patients (x^2 = 6.529; 1 df; two tails; $0.01 < p < 0.02$). (See fig. 1.)

Fatalities were slightly, but not significantly, more elevated among men (28.6%) than among women (11.1%), but the males with susto were, in most cases, slightly older than their female counterparts.

Information on the official cause of death was available in only five cases, although there was no medical certification in any of the eight fatalities. One subject was reported to have died "from a cough"; another from an embolism (without indication of location); one woman was accidentally shot with a firearm; another died as a result of a beating by her husband; and the last death was attributed to susto itself. These explanations of death, and our data from seven years before, are insufficient to determine the "real" cause of death, its relationship to the earlier diagnoses, or to the role of susto in the evolution of each case that ended in death. We speculatively ask three questions: Is there some way in which susto functions as a cause of death? How can susto and violent death be related? And, finally, does susto represent a refuge for patients who have otherwise lost hope? In introducing these issues, we make no attempt to prove anything conclusively, inasmuch as we do not have the material to do so. We do offer some speculations, which may provide some insight into these issues.

Can susto in some way cause a patient's demise? The answer from the people themselves is a resounding "yes," and from the local civil authorities it is also clearly affirmative, as shown by the information collected from divers informants, as well as from the Civil Registry in the Zapotec community. Can something further be deduced from the present study?

The person whose official cause of death was listed as susto had been examined by us in 1971. She was a Chinantec woman, 30 years of age in 1971, who complained of a "lump in the stomach," which she had suffered for approximately one year before the history was taken. It caused her pain, especially when her husband experienced difficulties with their neighbors.

She was found to be suffering from dysuria, migraine headaches, and debility. Moreover, she reported fits of rage and of weeping, nervousness, ill humor, weakness, and sweaty hands. She had borne seven children of which six had died, four at birth and the other two later, of measles and diarrhea. Her mother had died in childbirth, leaving the patient with three, apparently healthy, siblings. Upon asking her to what she attributed her complaints, she responded, "It's that neighbors come over to our house and they want to insult and physically attack my husband, and I become frightened ("yo me asusto"). The first time was in 1968, next it was in 1969, and again in 1970. It's due to their envy ("envidia"). (See Foster 1965; Rubel 1977.) In May of this year it returned, and I again suffered susto ("me asusté")."

The physical examination failed to reveal a tumor or any other explanation for the lump of which she complained. Her blood pressure was 120/100, pulse was 104 per minute, and oral temperature was 37.3° C. No pathology of any kind was found. The laboratory reported a count of 11.1 gr. percent for hemoglobin, 4.2 million red blood cells per m.1. and 37 percent of hematocrit. The white blood cells were 5,700 per m.1., with lymphatisis at 40 percent. Sedimentation was 3 mm per hour. Giardia lamblia was found in her stool. The clinical scorers made diagnoses of arterial hypertension, anemia, chronic colitis, and psychoneurosis.

In the absence of other data, we suggest the possibility that her arterial hypertension worsened and, because she did not obtain proper treatment, the patient succumbed.

The role of susto as a first and principal contributing cause of a victim's death is more in evidence in the case of Rogelio, another Chinantec who, in 1971, was 57 years old. (His clinical record can be found in chapter III.) Following the killing of his son, his life had oscillated between sadness and apathy until it took a dramatic turn for the worse in 1970. (We took his history in 1971.) One day in 1970, after the physical exertion of carrying a load of corn, he felt pain in his body and a "burning in his heart" [pointing to the right side of his abdomen]. He consulted a physician who told him he suffered from liver problems and treated him, but some time afterward he suffered a bout of diarrhea and worsened; he lost his "strength" (*fuerza*) and appetite, and his entire body swelled.

His history showed a man who, from the time he lost his

son, lost interest in work and began the slow march to death. Neither his physicians nor the curandero (healer) could deflect him from that path. The patient considered his condition was caused by muina (repressed anger), but the curandero treated him on the assumption it was susto. The weakness and other symptoms give an impression fitting the clinical picture of susto, but traditional treatment produced only a temporary remission. The critical issue is whether the problem for which he was treated determined the gravity of his condition and ultimate demise. Would he have suffered so grievously if his son had continued by his side, or if he simply hadn't been killed? His medical history suggests not. Independent of the cause of death, susto made the difference between a reportedly good state of health and the initiation of a long process terminating in death.

One Zapotec asustado, Rafael (who was 66 years old in 1971), had an affliction which continued for seven years. We diagnosed it as pulmonary in nature, probably tuberculosis. He had 11.7 gr. percent of hemoglobin, with 4.2 million red blood cells per m.l., and a hematocrit level of 36 percent. White blood cells were 7,600 per m.l. with neutrophilia at 82 percent. Sedimentation of 46 mm in an hour (corrected to 26). Evidence of *Entamoeba Histolytica* and *Trichomona intestinalis* was found in his stool. Tuberculosis was not confirmed, but the patient died some time later. According to official records, he died "from a cough."

In summary, the relationship between susto and death falls into two parts. The first is the statistical correlation between susto and the likelihood of death, which is far higher than in the absence of susto. The second shows the effect of susto on the death rate from diseases from which the patient is suffering simultaneously. Inclusion of susto in a patient's medical history tips the balance towards death.

Finally, our results did not permit classification of susto as a disease entity according to criteria used by biomedicine. We cannot report a specific etiology (a germ, for example) or a singular physiopathology (e.g., an attack on an organ or on a specific system). Instead, the findings point toward a condition that attacks patients in a diffuse, generalized fashion, to which insult the individual responds by nonspecific symptoms indicating organic and psychoemotional distress. Susto increases the risk of a patient dying by exacerbating the consequences of those organic diseases which are endemic to these rural communities.

6

Interrelationships Among Results

AT the beginning of this research, we planned to collect data with several questions in mind.

1. In communities in which the culture links onset of a folk illness to a frightening event, what distinguishes those who fall victim from those who do not?
2. For those who fall ill, what consequences do they suffer?
3. Among the victims, why are some more seriously affected than others?

These questions raise an issue that has interested anthropologists and health researchers for many years: how are we to comprehend people of other cultures when they complain of being sick and attribute their condition to causes that do not "fit" our medical concepts? These Oaxacan villagers explain the susto condition as due to an essential part of the person becoming separated from the body. Among the Mestizos, this essence is simply lost or wandering freely, whereas among the two Indian groups it has been captured by spirit beings, denizens of the natural environment, and is being held for expiation.

Since our own understandings of an individual's illness did not include separation of spirit from body, nor did we accept attribution of sickness to supernatural beings, we were left ill equipped to work with such presumptions. On the contrary, these were the very premises on which the villagers based their explanation of the susto problem!

On yet another level of understanding, an important difference between the villagers' interpretation of susto and our own was that they attributed the onset of the condition to one or several uncommon, frightening events. Thus, one of the women attributed her lack of well-being to an occasion when her clothing and residence caught fire; a man to having sighted a snake; a woman to having been swept away by a river current; and another man to having been threatened by machete-wielding acquaintances. On the contrary, we hypothesized that the stressors in these instances reflected more mundane, everyday reality—that they were the consequences of a person's unsatisfactory performance of roles as measured against his or her own standards. We found that these occasions were not unusual or equally distressing to all those experiencing them. That is, although everyone subscribed to the cultural understanding, not everyone proved susceptible, and the effects of becoming asustado varied from one victim to another. We assumed that the more often some individuals experienced inadequacy of role performance the more cumulative the effect, and the more likely he or she would complain of being asustado.

We used an open-system model to emphasize interactions among the social, emotional, and biological dimensions of individuals living in rural Oaxaca. The model was especially useful in the identification and definition of a problem familiar only to lay persons whose concepts of etiology and illness differ from our own. Whereas the villagers "knew" susto to be a sickness, we were obliged to consider the possibility that it was, instead, a stylized pattern of behavior by which individuals attempted to correct troublesome social relations, or to call attention to their social or emotional needs. To find which of these alternative explanations best interpreted our information, we approached the issue by thinking of susto as a problem, a lack of well-being, a difficulty, but *not* as a sickness, a disease, or an illness. That is, we worked with terms that subsumed illness and disease, as well as other difficulties; we refrained from the use of terms that would a priori exclude causes of suffering other than disease and illness.

In the interest of obtaining as clear a picture as possible of the different dimensions of a person suffering susto, tests were developed to probe in each of three areas: social role performance, psychiatric impairment, and organic disease. To advance this probing, three alternative hypotheses were posed:

1. Persons actively complaining of being asustado are performing social roles less adequately according to their own criteria than others of the same community.
2. Persons with susto are suffering higher levels of psychiatric impairment than others similar to them.
3. Asustados are more organically diseased than those with whom they are compared.

We predicted that only the social role hypothesis would receive support and the other two would be disconfirmed. We further anticipated that, although there would be some interaction between the three dimensions, the second two hypotheses would not receive support and could be laid to rest. Tests were fashioned to probe, independently of one another, the association between being asustado and identifiable problems in each of the respective dimensions: social, emotional, and organic.

Our results supported the first, and major, hypothesis—susto was associated with a person's perception of his or her inadequacy in the performance of critical social roles. The second hypothesis, as tested by the 22-Item Screening Score, received no support. The third hypothesis did receive unexpected support. Asustados suffered more disease signs and symptoms than their matched controls and these were more impairing and life-threatening. On the other hand, no single condition or system involvement differentiated between the two groups with one interesting exception. That exception referred to the aggregation of symptoms—lack of appetite, tiredness, loss of weight, loss of strength, and lack of motivation—that were reported so often in association with divers serious health problems. This aggregate was the only marker of organic difficulties that unambiguously distinguished the asustados from those patients without susto. Thus, in a universe of sick individuals, asustados were significantly more afflicted than others by a cluster of symptoms representing diffuse systematic attacks on the organism (cf. Fabrega 1970). That finding was the more remarkable because it corroborated the villagers' own reports that these are what constituted the core of the classic susto syndrome in Mexico and in other Latin American countries. Other than the aggregation of symptoms just discussed, none of the other organic symptoms, signs, or diagnoses discriminated successfully between the asustado and the control groups. On the contrary, clinical impressions of greater emotional difficulties did discriminate between the two groups. Although differences in number of clinically perceived emotional problems were at respectable levels of significance, these represented but 6 percent of total pathology. There were also such dramatic differences in judgment between the two physician evaluators that concern and uncertainty about the meaning of those results was felt. (We discussed this problem in greater detail at the beginning of this chapter.)

Discovery that the daily activities of patients complaining of susto were more restricted than those of the other patients was found to be not simply because they suffered more pathology. Results of the qualitative assessment of their pathological conditions were equally useful. Although suffering from the kinds of diseases common to these rural populations, assessments as to length of time symptoms had been present, their aggregate damage to the organism, the manner in which one problem made the organism more susceptible to other insults, provided a clinical judgment independent of the *number* of difficulties reported.

The panel of physician-scorers also assessed the likelihood that a patient's composite clinical picture was life-threatening. This assessment showed that, both quantitatively and qualitatively, those whose clinical picture included susto would be more likely to die as a result of their condition. In fact, during the seven-year period following collection of these data, 8 of the 47 asustados followed up did die, whereas *none* of the other patients followed up succumbed. The predictive association between scores on the gravity measure and the actual fatality rate is noteworthy. This association did not, however, predict what the patient would die of. What could be predicted was that someone with a high gravity score suffered problems that were clearly of such a nature—numerically and qualitatively—as to endanger his or her life. It was this gestalt assessment that permitted understanding of why the five fatalities for which we had a cause of death were attributed to so wide a range of problems. If *only* organic pathology had been taken into account, it would have proven difficult to find the common thread that linked these officially registered "causes of death." The holistic approach informed us that, although those who did die were sicker than others, they suffered from remarkably diverse problems. That discovery helped us better comprehend the improbable connection between deaths caused by violent acts and those more clearly related to disease processes.

What were some of the ties among the several problematic dimensions tested? It seemed reasonable to expect, for example, that difficulties assessed by the social stress measure would also be reflected in the psychiatric sphere. The reader will recall that the modified screening score for psychiatric impairment had failed to discriminate between those patients with susto and those without. Those results (tables 4 and 5) did not lead us to anticipate a relationship between these measures.

It was surprising to find a positive—but not universally significant—correlation. We found it plausible inasmuch as some level of psychiatric distress could be expected when individuals felt themselves socially stressed. In other words, something that was nonspecifically "psychological" had to exist in each of the two independent measures.

The Social Stress Gauge was not constructed to identify that component. The implication was that higher levels of social stress implied higher levels of psychological distress. The "psychological overlap" component was, we assumed, measured

TABLE 14

CORRELATIONS BETWEEN SOCIAL STRESS AND SEVERITY OF ILLNESS

Culture	Controls			Asustados		
	r_s	t	Probability Level	r_s	t	Probability Level
Chinantec	0.5	2.47	≤0.05*	0.3	1.23	>0.20†
Zapotec	0.5	1.5	>0.20†	0.2	0.5	>0.20†
Mestizo	0.2	1.56	>0.10†	0.3	1.33	>0.20†

Spearman Rho Test

* Significant at ≤0.05, two tails.
† Not significant.

symptomatically by the 22-Item Screening Score. We also assumed that each of these independent evaluations differentially revealed the "psychological overlap" they shared.

Various diagnostic efforts found asustados to be more organically diseased than controls. However, it should be remembered that the measures of severity did not distinguish statistically between the two samples, whereas gravity did (table 12). Nevertheless, we felt that we should examine possible relationships between the social stress and severity of illness measures. Our negative findings are presented in table 14.

The only correlation uncovered in those findings of sufficient magnitude to be statistically significant was one found among controls in the Chinantec community. Given its isolation, it may represent nothing more than a random occurrence; however, it may be relevant to the finding that muscular–skeletal conditions figured more prominently in the complaints of Chinantec controls than among asustados. (See table 10.) Inasmuch as muscular–skeletal conditions contribute considerable weight to the severity of illness measure, clinical interpretation of why those complaints were more frequently associated with controls than with asustados would be helpful.

A general interpretation of the findings in table 14 is simply that there was no demonstratable association between what was measured by the Social Stress Gauge and what was assessed by the severity measure.

Contrary to the predictions of the anthropologists, the gravity of disease measure found asustados to score higher than controls. The findings were statistically significant in three of the five tests that were run (table 12).

Since both the social stress measure and the gravity of disease measure were found to be positively associated with the susto condition, we felt that a strong correlation might be detected between these two measures. A correlational test was carried out with results presented in table 15.

However, those findings indicated an absence of association between social stress and gravity of disease. The two measures appear truly independent of one another, and each assesses a distinct dimension of the susto phenomenon. The measures were, of course, designed to be independent of one another, the intention being to evaluate discrete problem dimensions associated with being asustado.

Because we found a lack of correlation between these assessments can we then assume no possible link between the phenomenon each was designed to measure? We think not. Instead, the link lies in the meaning of social stressors and in how they are implicated in the susto condition. We still do not understand

TABLE 15

CORRELATIONS BETWEEN SOCIAL STRESS AND GRAVITY OF ILLNESS

Culture	Controls			Asustados		
	r_s	t	Probability Level	r_s	t	Probability Level
Chinantec	0.3	1.15	>0.20†	0.4	1.75	>0.05†
Zapotec	0.6	1.92	>0.05†	0.2	0.49	>0.20†
Mestizo	−0.2	0.75	>0.20†	−0.01	0.04	>0.20†

Spearman Rho Test

† Not significant.

why both social stress and gravity of disease are associated with susto complaints and not associated with one another. Similar puzzling results are reported by other stress researchers (McGrath 1970:12–13).

One must guard against an overly simplistic interpretation of the relationships among mind, body, and social dimensions in any evaluation of relative states of well-being. As indicated elsewhere, we express bemusement, not dismay, at the lack of correlation between a social stress score and measures of gravity of disease (O'Nell, Rubel, and Collado 1978).

Unfortunately, this research was not organized to provide historical depth, nor did it lend itself to sequential analysis of the several problems affecting the asustados. It was difficult to discern from these results whether susto victims became seriously diseased first and then experienced a drop in role performance or whether they performed unsatisfactorily first and then suffered health impairments. As noted earlier in the folk explanation, the great variability in time elapsing between the frightening event that precipitated the susto and the onset of signs and symptoms made a sequential analysis even more problematic. Nonetheless, some inferences of a temporal nature were possible.

Longitudinal information was available in responses to some of the questions on the Social Stress Gauge. For example, we found that an adult who had not completed the number of years of formal schooling he or she thought essential had been suffering from that discrepancy for a number of years. For those who considered it necessary to own plow animals but failed to possess them, the consequences of that incongruence had been cumulating over the years. Similarly, women who experienced difficulties in bearing children or nurturing them through infancy provided a time depth not otherwise available. These sequential data suggested that an individual's sense of social inadequacy probably preceded the onset of disease. Acknowledging to himself that he is not meeting his own standards of performance in critical tasks apparently makes a person's body even more vulnerable to endemic disease, a sequence that has dangerous consequences for overall well-being—socio-economic, organic, and emotional. To suffer from susto is to suffer a deterioration in overall well-being.

The associations we have reported are only that. They do not suggest that one or more sustos *cause* an increase in number of symptoms, or exacerbation of severity, or that they bring about the asustado's demise. However, there remains no doubt that susto greatly increases the probability of grievous deterioration in health, and eventual death.

Our results confirmed an interaction among the complaint of susto, inadequacy in the performance of social role, and a heavier than ordinary disease load. Suffering susto adds to the already heavy burden of disease commonly experienced by Oaxacan villagers. Clearly, it did not require an interdisciplinary project like this one to point out that Oaxacan villagers bore more than their share of disease. It was only by means of such an investigation, however, that some peasants were identified as more diseased than others and that that difference was associated with the susto condition.

Implications of This Study

The value of taking an interdisciplinary approach to problems of well-being in other cultures is strongly affirmed by these results. We began with a social anthropological question seeking the relationship between social role performance and the susto condition. Subsequent inclusion of a physician in the research group provided new perspectives, added clinical questions, and obliged us to consider interactions between clinical and social phenomena which we had not expected. Asking uncommon questions produced unexpected information about the susto phenomenon. This new information carries important implications for both social scientists and clinicians.

Susto poses a challenge to cosmopolitan medicine: it demands of the clinician an understanding of its cause, its dynamics, and the means of prevention. It is dangerous to the health of the individual and, consequently, detrimental to the well-being of society.

We have shown that the presence of susto demonstrably adds to an already heavy burden of disease among rural Mexicans. For practitioners the message is clear: if a patient includes susto in the presenting complaint, he or she is more likely to be overwhelmed by the overall clinical problems, less able to cope with obligations, and less capable of earning a living or otherwise contributing to maintenance of the family. Such physical exhaustion and its accompanying lack of ordinary motivation to accomplish daily tasks should cause attending physicians alarm and alert them to a potentially life-threatening situation.

The results have important implications for anthropology as well. They show the fruitfulness of a search for cross-cultural generalizations about a clearly defined phenomenon in a culture area in which substantial ethnographic background is already available. Under such benevolent circumstances, controlled comparisons can produce generalizations across a range of similar societies. Our own efforts were encouraged by the already solid ethnographic base provided by earlier studies of the health dimensions of Mexican cultures (Aguirre Beltrán 1963; Carrasco 1960; Foster 1951; and others).

The results demonstrate the value of analyzing how patients afflicted by a folk condition act out being ill as opposed to simply providing a description of how a group understands and explains it. We assumed that, in any society, difficulties that caused suffering or impairment would be responded to actively, not fatalistically, and that that behavior would be susceptible to description, comparison, and analysis (Kluckhohn 1953:509–510). We assumed that when disease was involved some of the victim's response would be generated by the pathology itself, relatively free of cultural guidance, and that it would prove rewarding to probe for it. The effort bore fruit.

Because we used the methodology of cross-cultural, controlled comparison, our results took us beyond how residents of one small and culturally specific municipio in Mexico coped with a problem. Our findings transcend cultural boundaries, applying equally well to three groups with distinctive languages, cultures, and social histories. We now understand better some of the ways that social, biological, and emotional systems of rural Mexicans respond to trying circumstances.

Although the hypothesized relationship between a susto complaint and a victim's inadequate level of role performance was demonstrated, it proved insufficient to explain susto. Finding that asustados also suffered an uncommonly heavy burden of biological disease obliged us to reappraise the premises with which we began. Now it is inadequate and inappropriate to conceive of susto as a form of unique social behavior on the one hand, or as a purely biomedical phenomenon on the other. Before collection of these data, we had argued (Rubel 1964:280; O'Nell and Selby 1968:97; O'Nell 1972:4) that a susto complaint simply legitimized "time off" from the exigencies of everyday roles, and we found Uzzell's (1974) application of the sick-role concept persuasive and helpful. However, our new findings demonstrate that the life burdens of ordinary Oaxacans overburden the asustados. Doubly taxed by a perceived inability to perform critical role assignments and an excessive load of disease, the asustado finds it impossible to carry out his normal responsibilities. Rather than electing the sick role to legitimize a respite from their obligations, asustados are *forced to the sidelines* by excessive demands on their adaptive resources.

It remains a theoretical possibility that other folk illnesses could be credibly explained as either uniquely social or uniquely biological processes. Such a conclusion must, however, remain in doubt until empirical research has taken the other, rival possibility into account and seriously probed its explanatory value. As our results demonstrate, the most fruitful approach to understanding folk illnesses is to seek an interaction between social and biological factors.

Appendix

22-Item Screening Score for Measuring Psychiatric Impairment (Modified)

1. Do you feel tired most of the time?

   Yes _____
   No _____
   Don't know _____

2. Are there many times when you don't feel like doing anything?

   Yes _____
   No _____
   Don't know _____

3. How do you feel most of the time? Happy, variable, worried?

   Happy _____
   Variable _____
   Worried _____
   Don't know _____

4. Do you often feel that others are not helpful enough?

   Yes _____
   No _____
   Don't know _____

5. Are you ever troubled by your heart beating very strongly and quickly?

   Often _____
   Sometimes _____
   Never _____
   Don't know _____

6. Do you usually enjoy eating?

   Yes _____
   No _____
   Don't know _____

7. Are there times when you feel so nervous that you can't remain in one place for a long period?

   Yes _____
   No _____
   Don't know _____

8. Do you consider yourself a worrier?

Yes _____
No _____
Don't know ___

9. When you become annoyed with someone, do you feel your breathing become more rapid?

Often _____
Sometimes ____
Never _____
Don't know ___

10. When someone annoys you, do you speak to them about it?

Yes _____
No _____
Don't know ___

11. Have you lost consciousness because of a strong reaction to something?

Yes _____
No _____
Don't know ___

12. Have you had problems in going to sleep, or remaining asleep?

Yes _____
No _____
Don't know ___

13. If a drunk affronts you, do you become angry?

Yes _____
No _____
Sometimes ____
Don't know ___

14. Do you often forget things?

Yes _____
No _____
Don't know ___

15. Have you suffered chills or hot and cold flashes?

Yes _____
No _____
Don't know ___

16. When troubled by problems, do your hands tremble?

Often _____
Sometimes ____
Never _____
Don't know ___

17. When troubled do you seek advice?

Almost always _____
Sometimes ____
Never _____
Don't know ___

18. Do your family problems tire you
    or cause you sickness?

    Yes _____
    No _____
    Don't know ___

19. Do you feel alone even while in the
    company of others from your
    community?

    Often _____
    Sometimes _____
    Never _____
    Don't know ___

20. For you, do things result as you
    wish them to?

    Often _____
    Sometimes _____
    Never _____
    Don't know ___

21. Do you get headaches when you
    must make a decision?

    Often _____
    Sometimes _____
    Never _____
    Don't know ___

22. For you, how does life treat you:
    well, all right, sadly?

    Well _____
    All right _____
    Sadly _____
    Don't know ___

Instructions for Scoring the 22-Item Screening Score Responses

A. 1. Indicate on the mimeographed scoring sheets the place, name, and number of the protocol you are currently scoring.
   2. The scorer should indicate his name, or code number, and the date of scoring on the score sheet.
   3. All items *must* be scored. Appropriate scores for each item are: 0, 0.5, 1. Those scores must be placed in the space provided immediately to the right of the item being scored.
   4. If the scorer has a problem or a question about how to score an item, or if he finds it necessary to comment in

some way about an item, this should be indicated by a checkmark in the space allocated for "Comment."

5. Please *refrain* from summing the item scores until decisions can be arrived at with respect to the best way to score items 10 and 13.

6. Please do not mark anything in the "Corrected Score" space.

7. If *more* than 5 items have been scored as "No sabe," this should be noted in the space allocated to "General Comments"; other general comments are to be noted there as well.

B. Scoring is to be as follows:

1. Yes = 1	No = 0	Don't know = 0.5	
2. Yes = 1	No = 0	Don't know = 0.5	
3. Happy = 0	Variable = 0.5	Worried = 1	Don't know = 0.5
4. Yes = 1	No = 0	Don't know = 0.5	
5. Often = 1	Sometimes = 0.5	Never = 0	Don't know = 0.5
6. Yes = 0	No = 1	Don't know = 0.5	
7. Yes = 1	No = 0	Don't know = 0.5	
8. Yes = 1	No = 0	Don't know = 0.5	
9. Often = 1	Sometimes = 0.5	Never = 0	Don't know = 0.5
10. Yes = 0	No = 1	Don't know = 0.5	
11. Yes = 1	No = 0	Don't know = 0.5	
12. Yes = 0	No = 1	Don't know = 0.5	
13. Yes = 1	No = 0	Sometimes = 0.5	Don't know = 0.5
14. Yes = 1	No = 0	Don't know = 0.5	
15. Often = 1	No = 0	Don't know = 0.5	
16. Often = 1	Sometimes = 0.5	Never = 0	Don't know = 0.5
17. Almost always = 1	Sometimes = 0	Never = 0	Don't know = 0.5
18. Yes = 1	No = 0	Don't know = 0.5	
19. Often = 1	Sometimes = 0.5	Never = 0	Don't know = 0.5
20. Often = 0.5	Sometimes = 0	Never = 1	Don't know = 0.5
21. Often = 1	Sometimes = 0.5	Never = 0	Don't know = 0.5
22. Well = 0	All right = 0	Sadly = 1	Don't know = 0.5

Note: For accuracy when summing scores, always use 0.5 when called for, not .5!

C. It is an assumption of this scoring procedure that an intermediate, or N.S. (Don't know), response is indicative of a partial agreement with the thrust of the question. For the same reason, responses that are not called for in the instrument but which also indicate positions *between* stress and nonstress are to be scored 0.5.

Social Factors Questionnaire*

Place (town) _____

No. _____

I General Data

1. Complete name _____

2. Sex _____ 3. Age _____

4. Living with one's spouse? Yes _____ No _____

5. *Children*   *Sex*   *Age*

   _____   _____   _____

   _____   _____   _____

6. Total number of sons _____

   Total number of daughters _____

7. House size _____ House type _____

8. Additional observations concerning the house:

II Personal Information on the Individual Being Interviewed

1. Does he or she have physical or mental impairments which lead to failure in his/her social role? Describe here:

2. Is there any indication that this individual fails to maintain suitable relations with others in the community? Describe here:

3. With respect to his/her conduct does he/she behave adequately with neighbors and community members? Describe here:

Place (town) _____

No. _____

III *For Men Only*

1. Is it necessary to have animals in this town?

   Yes _____ No _____

*From "Social Stress Gauge," copyright 1976 by Carl W. O'Nell and Arthur J. Rubel.

2. Is it necessary to have a team of oxen in this town?

   Yes _____ No _____

3. How many years of "cargo" service should a man of your age have completed? _____

4. Should an individual consult with another person to resolve a domestic problem?

   Yes _____ No _____

5. When a person from here works as a field hand (for others), is it a good thing, is it simply all right, or is it unfortunate?

   Good _____ All right _____ Unfortunate _____

6. How much corn does a family such as yours need to harvest? _____

7. Is it important for a person in this town to know how to read and write?

   Yes _____ No _____

8. How many years of study are suitable for a farmer from here? _____

9. Is life more difficult for husbands or wives, or is it equally difficult for both?

   Husbands _____ Wives _____

   Equal (for both) _____

10. Is life more difficult for one before 40 years of age, or after 40?

    Before _____ After _____

11. Do your fellow townsmen/neighbors have great or little respect for you?

    Great _____ Little _____

12. Do your own children have great or little respect for you?

    Great _____ Little _____

13. Does your wife have great or little respect for you?

    Great _____ Little _____

14. What is the amount of corn consumed daily by your family? _____

15. From the time of Holy Week (or All Saints), have you done any of these things?
    a. Have you sold something in the market?   _____
    b. Have you tilled your own fields?   _____
    c. Have you discharged a "cargo" in the community?   _____
    d. Have you served on some committee —school, road, water committee, etc.?   _____
    e. Have your worked on some obligatory community project?   _____
    f. Have you worked away from the town?   _____
    g. Have you helped a close relative, neighbor, or *compadre* in his work?   _____
    h. Have you engaged in another task?   _____
16. Do your older children help you whenever possible?
    Always _____ Sometimes _____ Never _____
17. Of the offices that follow, which have you filled?
    a. policeman   _____
    b. police chief   _____
    c. sponsor of patron saint   _____
    d. first *regidor*   _____
    e. municipal president   _____
    f. committee president   _____
18. Of your offices and services, which were the last ones in which you served?
    1. _____ 2. _____
19. In which years did you serve them?
    1. _____ 2. _____
20. When you began living with your wife did you live in the house of your elders?
    Yes _____ No _____
    If the answer is yes, for how long?
    Less than 1 year _____ More than 1 year _____
    Place (town) _____
    No. _____

III *For Women Only*

1. Should an individual consult with another person to resolve a domestic problem?.

    Yes _____ No _____

2. When a person from here works as a field hand or a house servant (for others), is it a good thing, simply all right, or is it unfortunate?

    Good _____ All right _____

    Unfortunate _____

4. How much corn does a family such as yours need to harvest? _____

5. How many years of study are suitable for a country woman from here? _____

6. Is life more difficult for wives or husbands, or is it equally difficult for both?

    Husbands _____ Wives _____

    Equal (for both) _____

7. Is life more difficult for one before 40 years of age, or after 40?

    Before _____ After _____

8. Do other people in your town and your neighbors have great or little respect for you?

    Great _____ Little _____

9. Do your own children have great or little respect for you?

    Great _____ Little _____

10. Does your husband have great or little respect for you?

    Great _____ Little _____

11. What is the amount of corn consumed daily by your family? _____

12. From the time of Holy Week (or All Saints), have you done any of these things?

    a. Have you sold something in the market? _____

    b. Have you prepared food? _____

    c. Have you given birth? _____

    d. Have you made pottery, bread, or cheese? _____

e. Have you helped a close relative, a
   comadre, or a neighbor in her work? _____

f. Have you taken care of children? _____

g. Have you engaged in another task? _____

13. Of the things you have done, which is the one of which
    you are most proud? _____

14. In the task in which you have most pride, do you do it
    better than, equal to, or less well than other women in
    the town?

    Better than _____ Equal to _____

    Less well than _____

15. Is your father (or husband) satisfied with the work you
    do?

    Yes _____ No _____

16. Do your older children help you whenever possible?

    Always _____ Sometimes _____ Never _____

17. Of all your children, how many were born dead?

    _____

18. Have you nursed all your surviving children?

    Yes _____ No _____

19. Of all your children, living at the time of birth, can you
    tell me how many have died before attaining 3 years of
    age? _____

20. How do you perceive your tasks as wife and mother in
    your family?

    Very laborious? _____ Ordinary? _____

    Easy? _____

21. When you began to live with your husband, did you live
    in the house of your elders?

    Yes _____ No _____

    If the answer is yes, for how long?

    More than one year _____ Less than one year _____

    Place (town) _____

    No. _____

IV *For Both Men and Women*

1. To whom does this house belong?
   Husband _____ Wife _____ Another _____

2. For how many years have you gone to school?

   _____

3. Do you know how to read and write?

   Some _____ Scarcely _____

   Do not know how _____

4. Do you have a burro? _____ A horse? _____ An ox
   team? _____ A truck? _____ A bicycle? _____

5. A couple ought to live in the house of the man?
   _____ The woman? _____ No difference? _____

6. Over the last two years, have you worked as field hand
   or servant for others?

   Yes _____ No _____

7. When one's fellow townspeople or neighbors gossip about
   one, can a person live contentedly?

   Yes _____ No _____

8. For a person to live contentedly, is it necessary for him
   (or her) to have much or little respect (from others), or
   is that not important? Much _____ Little _____

   Not important _____

9. Of the following questions concerning life situations,
   can you tell me whether each one is serious, of little
   importance, or not at all significant?

   a. When a daughter elopes with her boyfriend, is the
      criticism that her parents endure for her serious?
      _____ Of little importance? _____

      Not at all significant? _____

   Have you experienced this misfortune? _____

   b. When a son elopes with his girlfriend, is the criticism
      his parents endure for him serious? _____ Of little
      importance? _____ Not at all significant? _____
      Have you experienced this misfortune? _____

   c. When a young woman becomes pregnant before mar-

riage, is the criticism her parents endure for her serious? _____Of little importance? _____
Not at all significant? _____ Have you experienced this misfortune? _____

   d. When their son is a drunkard, is the criticism his parents endure for him serious? _____ Of little importance? _____ Not at all significant? _____ Have you experienced this misfortune? _____

10. Since All Saints (Holy Week) or over the last 6 months, have you consulted with any other person to solve a household problem? Yes _____ No _____ With whom have you consulted? _____

11. What quantity of corn did you harvest last year?

_____

12. Is it a good thing when a husband tells his wife the amount of corn yielded by his harvest?

                 Yes _____ No _____

Scoring Instructions for the Social Factors Questionnaire for Males

I *Purpose and Rationale of the Questionnaire and Score Sheet*

   The joint use of the Social Factors Questionnaire and Score Sheet enables outside observers to transform verbal response data into numerical scores reliably. This will be useful in the computation of measures relating to factors of social stress. The basic purpose is to facilitate the derivation of a single measure of cognitive role stress from sets of items that reveal discrepancies between perceived ideal role expectations and perceived actual discharge of role obligations. Positive scores result when respondents' answers indicate deficiencies in their reported behavior or experiences as compared to stated cognitively ideal standards of behavior.

The Score Sheet has been designed to allow for the differential weighting of the various components that make up each item. The weighting is based on the ethnographic knowledge the researchers have of the communities included in the study. Scoring is therefore done with respect to the explicit instructions presented in the two following sections and, in cases of ambiguity, with recourse to the scoring rationale indicated above.

II *General Instructions*

1. Each Social Factors Questionnaire requires the use of a separate Score Sheet.

2. Write your name, or code number if given one, in the upper right-hand corner of the Score Sheet. Also indicate the date on which the scoring is done under your name or number.

3. Transcribe *place, number, name, sex,* and *age* of person being interviewed from the Questionnaire to the Score Sheet.

4. Do not enter anything in the space provided for an ID Code.

5. Items are numbered sequentially within sections. Note that in all sections except Section A, each item is divided into idea (a) and actual (b) measures. Immediately following each Score item number is a combined number enclosed in parentheses. The Roman numeral style number refers to the various sections of the Questionnaire. The Arabic numeral refers to the Questionnaire item in that section. A few Score items also refer to subitems in the Questionnaire designated with letters, a, b, c, etc. N.B. Score sheets for males are scored with reference to Questionnaire section III, entitled *Solamente Para Señores.*

6. Scoring judgments for each Score item are made with reference to the Questionnaire items as indicated in (5), above.

7. Score items are scored first of all with respect to their components, as indicated in III, Item Instructions. Once all the components have been scored, the scorer derives

a score for each item in the space provided. Component scores may be checks or numbers. Item Scores are always numbers: 1, 2, or 0. The Grand Total is a number derived by adding all the item scores for a given Score Sheet.

8. For items with no response or a response that cannot be scored with the present instrument, do not score. Write in the number of the item under Remarks on the first page of the Score Sheet.

III *Item Instructions*

A. 1. Component scoring (I.4): If the respondent is not an adult, this item is not scored. If the respondent is an adult, does he have a spouse? Check Yes or No.

2. *Component scoring* (I.6.7.8): For Chinantecs, if the house type is adobe or *tabla*, check Yes. If the house type is *palito*, check No. For Zapotecs (I.8), adequate = yes; not adequate = no.

3. Component scoring (II.1): Any positive answer on this section of the Questionnaire is to be scored Yes with a check mark. A negative or no answer at all is to be scored No.

B. 1. a. *Component scoring* (III.1) (III.2): Check the proper response.

b. *Component scoring* (IV.4): If either a horse or burro or both are indicated, check Yes for *Has Animals.* Check other items as indicated.

2. a. *Component scoring* (III.6): Write in the amount of corn harvest as indicated by the respondent. Clearly indicate the measure as well as the number (kilo, *toneladas*, etc.).

b. *Component scoring* (IV.11): Write in the amount of the corn harvest as indicated by the respondent, with numbers and measure, as above.

3. a. *Component scoring* (III.7): Check Yes or No.

b. *Component scoring* (IV.3): Check Some, Little, or None.

4. a. *Component scoring* (III.8): Write in number of years

    indicated by the respondent.

    b. *Component scoring* (IV.2): Write in number of years indicated by the respondent.

C. 1. a. *Component scoring* (III.3): Write in number of years indicated by respondent.

    b. *Component scoring* (III.17): Write in number of years derived by summing up completed services to the community.

  2. a. *Component scoring* (III.3): Write in the number of years indicated by the respondent.

    b. *Component scoring* (III.15.c.d.e., III.18, III.19 and the marginal indications with III.17 are added to those services listed in III.17 to get a total number of years given to service in both the explicit and informal systems): If respondent indicates he has served more years than has been indicated in C.1.b., above, add this time to the time indicated in C.1.b. above.

  3. a. *Component scoring* (III): For Zapotecs. Indicate highest office should have held, in space provided. Also indicate highest office actually held, including present one, if applicable.

    b. *Component scoring* (III.18, III.19)

D. 1. a. *Component scoring* (III.4): Check Yes or No, as indicated by respondent.

    b. *Component scoring* (IV.10): Check Yes or No, as indicated by respondent. Indicate also the numbers of persons consulted.

  2. a. *Component scoring* (IV.8): Check level of respect, as indicated by the respondent.

    b. *Component scoring* (III.12, 13): Check each component in this item as it relates to the Questionnaire items, Much or Little.

  3. a. *Component scoring* (IV.9.a.b.c.d.): Indicate by numbers how many times each subitem is checked.

    b. *Component scoring* (IV.7): Check sensitivity to gossip, Yes or No. A No answer is indicative of sensitivity in this context.

E. 1. a. *Component scoring* (III.5): Check as indicated by the respondent. *Bueno* = positive; *regular* = neutral; *triste* = negative.

b. *Component scoring* (IV.6): Check Yes or No, as indicated by the respondent.

2. a. *Component scoring* (I.2): Check sex of the respondent.

b. *Component scoring* (III.9): Check Males, Females, or Equal, as indicated by the respondent.

3. a. *Component scoring* (I.3): Write in the age of the respondent.

b. *Component scoring* (III.10): Check Before 40 or After 40, as indicated by respondent. Also indicate if respondent is 40 years old.

4. a. *Component scoring* (IV.5): If respondent indicates *propria*, check Husband. If *señora*, check Wife. If *es igual*, check No Difference.

b. *Component scoring* (IV.1): If respondent indicates *propria*, check Husband. If *señora*, check Wife. If he indicates *otra*, check Some Other on the Score Sheet.

5. a. *Component scoring* For Chinantecs, write in 0. For Zapotecs, write in 2.

b. *Component scoring* (III.20): Check Yes or No, as indicated by respondent. If yes, check Less Than 1 Year or More Than 1 Year. Give number of years, if indicated.

6. a. *Component scoring*: For both Chinantecs and Zapotecs, indicate Yes.

b. *Component scoring* (III.16): Check as indicated by the respondent: Always, Sometimes, or Never.

7. a. *Component scoring* Disgrace is implied for Chinantecs and Zapotecs: Check Yes for these communities.

     b. *Component scoring* (IV.9.a.b.c.d.): Check each disgrace indicated by the respondent for None, Once, or Twice or more.

A. 1. *Item Scoring:* If respondent is not an adult, score 0. If respondent is an adult and Yes is checked, score 0. All No checks are scored 2.

  2. *Item Scoring:* Yes = 0; No = 2.

  3. *Item Scoring:* Yes = 2; No = 0.

B. 1. *Item Scoring:* If Yes for animals and oxen on both the ideal and actual components, score 0.

    If Yes for animals and oxen on the ideal components, but No for animals and oxen on actual components, score 2.

    If Yes for animals and oxen on the ideal components and one Yes and one No for these on the actual measure, score 1. If Yes on either of the ideals and No on both actuals, score 1.

    If No on both ideal components and No on the matching actual components, score 1.

    If Yes and No on the ideal components and Yes and No on the matching actual components, score 1.

    The indication of a truck and/or bicycle will reduce a 2 to a 1 and a 1 to 0, as scored above.

  2. *Item Scoring:* If (a) exceeds (b) by ⅓ or more, score 2.

    If (a) exceeds (b) by less than ⅓ so that (a) and (b) cannot be seen to approximate one another even roughly, score 1.

    If (a) and (b) are approximately equal or if (b) exceeds (a), score 0.

    (Note: One *tonelada* equals approximately 907 kilograms.)

  3. *Item Scoring:* If Yes for (a) and Some for (b), score 0.
If Yes for (a) and Little for (b), score 1.
If Yes for (a) and None for (b), score 2.
If No for (a) and None for (b), score 1.
If No for (a) and Some or Little for (b), score 0.

4. *Item Scoring:* If (a) and (b) are approximately equal, score 0.

   If (b) exceeds (a), score 0.

   If (a) exceeds (b) by one year, score 1.

   If (a) exceeds (b) by two or more years, score 2.

C. 1. *Item Scoring:* If (a) and (b) are equal, score 0.

   If (b) exceeds (a), score 0.

   If (a) exceeds (b) by one year, score 1.

   If (a) exceeds (b) by two or more years, score 2.

2. *Item Scoring:* If (a) and (b) are equal, score 0.

   If (b) exceeds (a) by one year, score 0.

   If (a) exceeds (b) by one year, score 1.

   If (a) exceeds (b) by more than two years, score 2.

3. *Item Scoring:* Use scale provided by the researcher to score this item.

D. 1. *Item Scoring:* If No for (a) and No for (b), score 0.

   If No for (a) and Yes for (b), score 2.

   If Yes for (a) and Yes for (b), score 1, if no more than one person is consulted.

   If Yes for (a) and Yes for (b), score 2, if two or more persons were consulted.

   If Yes for (a) and No for (b), score 0.

2. *Item Scoring:* If (a) is checked Much, and two or three answers in (b) are checked Little, score 2.

   If (a) is checked Much, and one answer in (b) is checked Little, score 1.

   If (a) is checked Little or No Importance, and (b) is checked Much, score 0.

   If both (a) and (b) are checked Little or No Importance, score 0.

3. *Item Scoring:* If three or more for Serious (3.a), and Yes for sensitivity (3.b.), score 2.

   If three or more for Serious, and No for sensitivity, score 1.

   If one or two Serious, and Yes for sensitivity, score 1.

If none for Serious, and No for sensitivity, score 0.

E. 1. *Item Scoring:* If (a) is Positive or Neutral, and (b) is Yes, score 1.

If (a) is Negative and (b) is Yes, score 2.

If (a) is Negative and (b) is No, score 0.

If (a) is Yes and (b) is Yes, score 1.

If (a) is Yes and (b) is No, score 0.

(Yes equals positive or neutral.)

2. *Item Scoring:* [when (a) is male]: if (b) is Males, score 2; if (b) is Equal, score 1; if (b) is Females, score 0.

3. *Item Scoring:* If (a) and (b) match, score 2.

If (a) and (b) do not match, score 0.

If (a) is 40 and (b) is After 40, score 1.

4. *Item Scoring:* If (a) checks Husband or No Difference, and (b) checks Husband, score 0.

If (a) checks Husband, and (b) indicates Wife or Some Other, score 2.

If (a) checks Wife and (b) checks Wife or Some Other, score 1.

If (a) is checked No Difference, and (b) is checked Some Other, score 0.

5. *Item Scoring* (For Chinantecs): If (b) is Yes and More Than One Year, score 1.

If (b) is Yes and Less Than One Year, score 0.

If (b) is No, score 0.

For Zapotecs, if (b) is Yes and More Than One Year, score 0.

If (b) is Yes and Less Than One Year, score 1.

If (b) is No, score 2.

6. *Item Scoring:* If (a) is Yes and (b) is Always, score 0.

If (a) is Yes and (b) is Sometimes, score 1.

If (a) is Yes and (b) is Never, score 2.

If (a) is No and (b) is Always, score 0.

If (a) is No and (b) is Sometimes or Never, score 1.

7. *Item Scoring:* Disgraced two or more times, score 2.

Disgraced once, score 1.

No disgrace, score 0.

Please total all item scores. The grand total constitutes the Social Factors Score for the individual. Enter this cumulative score as a Grand Total in the space provided.

Score Sheet for Social Factors Questionnaire—Males

Place: _____ Scorer's Name: _____
Number: _____ Scoring Date: _____
Name: _____ Remarks: _____
Sex: _____ Age: _____ ID Code: _____

Item
Scores

A. *Situational Factors*

   1. (I.4) Satisfactory conjugal
     relationship: Yes _____ No _____ _____

   2. (I.6.7.8) Adequate living
     conditions, given size and
     composition of family: Yes _____ No _____ _____

   3. (II.1) Physical or mental
     impediments to adequate
     social participation: Yes _____ No _____ _____

B. *Resources (Males)*

Ideal Measures

   1. a. (III.1) Animals necessary: Yes _____ No _____
      (II.2) Team of oxen
      necessary   Yes _____ No _____

Actual Measures

   1. b. (IV. 4) Has animals: Yes _____ No _____
      Has team of oxen: Yes _____ No _____
      Has truck: Yes _____ No _____
      Has bicycle: Yes _____ No _____

              Item Score: _____

Ideal Measures

   2. a. (III.6) Necessary amount
      of yearly corn
      harvest _____

Actual Measures

    2. b. (IV.11) Amount of yearly
          corn harvest _____

Item Score: _____

Ideal

    3. a. (III.7) Important to read
          and write: Yes _____ No _____

Actual

    3. b. (IV.3) Reads and writes:
          Some _____ Little _____
          None _____

Item Score: _____

Ideal

    4. a. (III.8) Number of years
          in school _____

Actual

    4. b. (IV.2) Number of years
          in school _____

Item Score: _____

C. *Community Service (Males)*

Ideal

    1. a. (III.3) Number of
          years _____

Actual

    1. b. (III.17) Number of
          years _____

Item Score: _____

Ideal

    2. a. (III.3) Number of
          years _____

Actual

    2. b. (III.17, III.15.c.d., III.18,
          III.19) Number of
          years _____

Item Score: _____

Ideal
    3. a. (III.3.) Highest office
           should have held _____

Actual
    3. b. (III.18, III.19.) Highest
           office actually held _____
                                      Item Score: _____

D. *Dependency of Others (Males)*
Ideal
    1. a. (III.4) Ought to consult
           with another: Yes _____ No _____

Actual
    1. b. (IV.10) Had consulted
           with another: Yes _____ No _____
                                  How many? _____
                                  Item Score: _____

Ideal
    2. a. (IV.8) Respect from
           others is desirable:
               Much _____ Little _____ No importance _____

Actual
    2. b. (III.11.12.13) Respect
           from townspeople/   Much _____ Little _____
           neighbors
           Own children   Much _____ Little _____
           Own wife   Much _____ Little _____
           Response ratio: _____ Score: _____
                                  Item Score: _____

Ideal
    3. a. (IV.9) Sensitivity to
           criticism of others:
           Serious _____ Light _____ Nothing _____
    3. b. (IV.7) Sensitivity to
           gossip: Yes _____ No _____
                                  Item Score: _____

E. *Personal Control of Affairs*
Ideal

    1. a. (III.5) Working for
            another:
            Positive _____ Neutral _____ Negative _____

Actual

    1. b. (IV.6) In last two years
            has worked for another: Yes _____ No _____

                                    Item Score: _____

Ideal

    2. a. (I.2) Sex of respondent:
            Male _____ Female _____

Actual

    2. b. (III.9) Life is more
            difficult for:
            Males _____ Females _____ Equal _____

                                    Item Score: _____

Ideal

    3. a. (I.3) Age of respondent _____

Actual

    3. b. Before 40 _____ After 40 _____ Equal _____
            Is respondent 40 or over? _____

                                    Item Score: _____

Ideal

    4. a. (IV.5) A pair should live
            in the house of:
            The Husband _____ The Wife _____ No Difference __

Actual

    4. b. (IV.1) Does the pair live
            in the house of:
            The Husband _____ The Wife _____ Some Other _____

                                    Item Score: _____

Ideal

    5. a. Ethnographic data: How

long should a young couple reside with parents before they establish their own house? _____

Actual

5. b. (III.20) Did the young couple (respondent) live with the parental pair: Yes _____ No _____
If yes, Less than
1 year _____
More than 1 year _____

Item Score: _____

Ideal

6. a. Ethnographic data: Should older children help their parents when possible? Yes _____ No _____

Actual

6. b. (III.16) Do your children help you as much as possible?
Always _____
Sometimes _____
Never _____

Item Score: _____

Ideal

7. a. Ethnographic data: Parental responsibility for the behavior of unmarried children is always marked Yes for Chinantecs and Zapotecs Yes _____ No _____

Actual

7. b. (IV.9.a.b.c.d.) Times disgrace is experienced by parent as result of child's behavior:
None _____
Once _____
Twice or
more _____

Item Score: _____
GRAND TOTAL: _____

Scoring Instructions for the
Social Factors Questionnaire for Females

I *Purposes and Rationale of the Questionnaire and Score Sheet*

The purpose and rationale of the Questionnaire and Score Sheet for Females is the same as that described in Section I of the *Scoring Instructions for the Social Factors Questionnaire for Males.*

II *General Instructions*

These instructions are the same as those provided in Section II of the *Scoring Instructions for the Social Factors Questionnaire for Males.*

III *Item Instructions*

    A. 1. *Component scoring* (I.4): If the respondent is not an adult (over 18), this item is not scored. If the respondent is an adult, does she have a spouse?
Check Yes or No.

      2. *Component scoring* (I.6.7.8): For Chinantecs, if house type is adobe or *tabla*, check Yes. If the house type is *palito*, check No. For Zapotecs (I.8), adequate = yes; not adequate = no.

      3. *Component scoring* (II.1): Any positive answer on this section of the Questionnaire is to be scored Yes with a check mark. A negative or no answer at all is to be scored No.

    B. 1. a. *Component scoring* (I.4): If woman has a spouse, check in space provided. (I.3): Indicate age of respondent.

        b. *Component scoring* (I.5.6): From information recorded for these items, indicate the total number of children a woman has.

      2. *Component scoring* (III.17): Write in the number of children who died at birth. (III.19): Write in the number of children who died before three years of age.

      3. a. *Component scoring:* For Chinantecs and Zapotecs, check Yes.

    b. *Component scoring* (III.18): Respondent nursed all of her infants. Indicate Yes or No.

4. *Component scoring* (III.12): Indicate total number of tasks reported.

5. a. *Component scoring* (III.13): Write in special task respondent says that she is proud of.

    b. *Component scoring* (III.14): Indicate level of competency.

6. a. *Component scoring* (IV.12): Should the husband inform his wife of the quantity of the corn harvest. Check Yes or No.

    b. *Component scoring* (III.4): Check Yes or No whether she indicates a knowledge of the amount of corn harvest.

7. a. *Component scoring:* For Chinantecs and Zapotecs, indicate Yes for responsibility.

    b. *Component scoring* (IV.9.a.b.c.d): Write in the number of times the respondent indicates she has been disgraced after Yes. If she reports none, check No.

8. *Component scoring* (III.20): Check Onerous, Moderate or Easy, as indicated by the respondent.

9. *Component scoring* (III.15): Check Yes or No, as indicated by the respondent.

C. 1. a. *Component scoring* (III.4): Write in the amount of the corn harvest indicated by the respondent. Indicate measures used, e.g., kilos, etc.

    b. *Component scoring* (IV.11): Write in the amount of corn reported actually to have been harvested using numbers and measures indicated by the respondent.

2. a. *Component scoring* (III.3): Check Yes or No.

    b. *Component scoring* (IV.3): Check Some, Little, or None.

3. a. *Component scoring* (III.5): Write in number of years indicated by the respondent.

    b. *Component scoring* (IV.2): Write in the number of years indicated by the respondent.

D. 1. a. *Component scoring* (III.1): Check Yes or No, as indicated by the respondent.

    b. *Component scoring* (IV.10): Check Yes or No; if yes, how many?

  2. a. *Component scoring* (IV.8): Check level of respect indicated.

    b. *Component scoring* (III.8.9.10): Indicate Much or Little respect from each category of person.

  3. a. *Component scoring* (IV.9): Check level of sensitivity.

    b. *Component scoring* (IV.7): Check Yes or No.

E. 1. a. *Component scoring* (III.2): Indicate response as Positive, Neutral, or Negative.

    b. *Component scoring* (IV.6): Check Yes or No.

  2. a. *Component scoring* (I.2): Check Female.

    b. *Component scoring* (III.6): Check Males, Females, or Equal.

  3. a. *Component scoring* (I.3): Indicate age of respondent.

    b. *Component scoring* (III.7): Indicate Before 40, After 40, or Equal.

  4. a. *Component scoring* (IV.5): Check Husband, Wife, or No Difference.

    b. *Component scoring* (IV.1): Check Husband, Wife, or Other.

  5. *Component scoring* (III.21): Check Yes or No. If yes, check Less Than or More Than one year. If time is indicated by respondent, write it in.

  6. b. *Component scoring* (III.16): Indicate Always, Sometimes, or Never.

A. 1. *Item scoring:* If respondent is not an adult, score 0. If adult and checked Yes, score 0.
All No checks are scored 2.

  2. *Item scoring:* Yes = 0; no = 2.

  3. *Item scoring:* Yes = 2; no = 0.

B. 1. *Item scoring:* If a woman has between three and eight children, is between the ages of 20 and 40, and has a spouse, score 0. If less than three, score 1; more than eight, score 2.

If a woman of any age has eight or more children but no spouse, score 2.

If a woman of over 25 has no child and no spouse, score 1.

2. *Item scoring:* If None in both categories, score 0.

   If one in either category, score 1.

   If two or more in one or both categories, score 2.

3. *Item scoring:* For Chinantecs and Zapotecs, score 0 if (b) is checked Yes. Score 2 if (b) is checked No.

4. *Item scoring:* If answer is five to seven tasks, score 0.

   If three to four tasks, score 1.

   If two or fewer tasks, score 2.

5. *Item scoring:* If (b) is answered Better Than or Equal To, score 0.

   If (b) is answered Less Than, score 2.

6. *Item scoring:* If (a) is Yes and (b) is Yes, score 0.

   If (a) is No and (b) is No, score 0.

   If (a) is Yes and (b) is No, score 2.

   If (a) is No and (b) is Yes, score 0.

7. *Item scoring:* (for Chinantecs and Zapotecs):

   If one disgrace, score 1.

   If more than one disgrace, score 2.

   If no disgrace, score 0.

8. *Item scoring:* If Onerous, score 2.

   If Moderate, score 1.

   If Easy, score 0.

9. *Item scoring:* Yes = 0

   No = 2

   Don't know = 1

C. 1. *Item scoring:* If (a) exceeds (b) by 1/3 or more, score 2. If (a) exceeds (b) by less than 1/3 so that (a) and (b) cannot be seen to approximate one another even roughly, score 1.

   If (a) and (b) are approximately equal or if (b) exceeds (a), score 0.

   (Note: One *tonelada* equals approximately 907 kilograms.)

2. *Item scoring:* If Yes for (a) and Some for (b), score 0.
   If Yes for (a) and Little for (b), score 1.
   If Yes for (a) and None for (b), score 2.
   If No for (a) and None for (b), score 1.
   If No for (a) and Some or Little for (b), score 0.

3. *Item scoring:* If (a) and (b) are approximately equal, score 0.
   If (b) exceeds (a), score 0.
   If (a) exceeds (b) by one year, score 1.
   If (a) exceeds (b) by two or more years, score 2.

D. 1. *Item scoring:* If No for (a) and No for (b), score 0.
   If No for (a) and Yes for (b), score 2.
   If Yes for (a) and Yes for (b), score 1 if no more than one is consulted.
   If Yes for (a) and Yes for (b), score 2 if two or more persons are consulted.

2. *Item scoring:* If (a) is checked Much, and two or three answers in (b) checked Little, score 2.
   If (a) is checked Much, and one answer in (b) is checked Little, score 1.
   If (a) is checked Much, and all three answers in (b) are checked Much, score 0.
   If (a) and (b) are both checked Little or No Importance, score 0.

3. *Item scoring:* If three or more indications of Serious in (a), and Yes (equals No on Questionnaire) for sensitivity, score 2.
   If three or more for Serious and No for sensitivity, score 2.
   If three or more for Serious and No for sensitivity, score 1.
   If one or two Serious, and Yes for sensitivity, score 1.
   If none for Serious, and Yes for sensitivity, score 0.
   If none for Serious, and No for sensitivity, score 0.

E. 1. *Item scoring:* If (a) is Positive or Neutral, and (b) is Yes, score 1.

If (a) is Negative and (b) is Yes, score 2.

If (a) is Negative and (b) is No, score 0.

If (a) is Yes and (b) is Yes, score 1.

If (a) is Yes and (b) is No, score 0.

2. *Item scoring:* If (b) is Females, score 2.

   If (b) is equal, score 1.

   If (b) is males, score 0.

3. *Item scoring:* If (a) is less than 40 years and (b) is Before, score 2.

   If (a) is 40 or more years and (b) is After, score 2.

   If (b) is Equal, score 1.

   If (a) is Less Than 40 years and (b) is After, score 0.

   If (a) is 40 or more and (b) is Before, score 0.

4. *Item scoring:* If (a) is Husband and (b) is Wife or Other, score 2.

   If (a) is Wife and (b) is Husband or Wife, score 1.

   If (a) is No Difference, score 0.

   If (a) is Husband and (b) is Husband, score 0.

5. *Item scoring* (for Chinantecs): If No, score 0.

   If Yes, and Less Than one year, score 0.

   If Yes, and More Than one year, score 1.

   (For Zapotecs): If No, score 2.

   If Yes and Less Than one year, score 1.

   If Yes and More Than one year, score 0.

6. *Item scoring* (for Chinantecs and Zapotecs):

$$\text{Always} = 0$$
$$\text{Sometime} = 1$$
$$\text{Never} = 2$$

Total up all Item Scores. Enter this total as the Grand Total score. It constitutes the Social Factors Score for the individual.

Score Sheet for Social Factors Questionnaire—
Females

Place: _____   Scorer's Name: _____

Number: _____   Scoring Date: _____

Name: _____   Remarks: _____

Sex: _____ Age: _____ ID Code: _____

					Item Scores

A. *Situational Factors*

    1. (I.4) Satisfactory conjugal relationship: Yes _____ No _____ _____

    2. (I.6.7.8) Adequate living conditions, given size and composition of family: Yes _____ No _____ _____

    3. (II.1) Physical or mental impediments to adequate social participation: Yes _____ No _____ _____

B. *Family Obligations (Females)*

Ideal Measures

    1. a. (I.4) Living with spouse

    _____

    (I.3) Age _____

Actual Measures

    1. b. (I.5.6) Number of children

    _____

        Item Score: _____

    2. a. (III.17) Number who died at birth _____

       b. (III.19) Number who died before 3 years of age _____

        Item Score: _____

Ideal Measures

    3. a. (For Chinantecs and Zapotecs) Is it considered important to nurse own children   Yes _____ No _____

Actual Measures

    3. b. (III.18) Nursed all viable
         children: Yes _____ No _____

                                         Item Score: _____

    4. (III.12) How many tasks
       done _____

                                         Item Score: _____

Ideal Measures

    5. a. (III.13) Special task _____

Actual Measures

    5. b. (III.14) Level of
         competency _____

                                         Item Score: _____

Ideal Measures

    6. a. (IV.12) Husband informs
         wife of quantity of harvest?   Yes _____ No _____
      b. (III.4) Does she know the
         amount of the corn
         harvest?   Yes _____ No _____

                                         Item Score: _____

Ideal Measures

    7. a. Mothers have some
         responsibility for behav-
         ior of unmarried children
         in both Chinantec and
         Zapotec villages.

Actual Measures

    7. b. (IV.9.a.b.c.) Disgrace at
         children's behavior:
         Yes (how many?) _____ No _____

                                         Item Score: _____

    8. (III.20) Tasks as wife and
       mother are perceived as: Onerous _____
                                   Moderate _____
                                   Easy _____

                                         Item Score: _____

9. (III.15) Is significant male satisfied with woman's work? Yes _____ No _____

Item Score: _____

C. *Resources (Females)*

Ideal Measure

1. a. (III.4) Yearly corn harvest needed _____

Actual Measure

1. b. (IV.11) Yearly corn harvest obtained _____

Item Score: _____

Ideal Measure

2. a. (III.3) Importance of reading and writing: Yes _____ No _____

Actual Measure

2. b. (IV.3) Do you read and write?

Some _____ Little _____ None _____

Item Score: _____

Ideal Measure

3. a. (III.5) Number of years should be in school _____

Actual Measure

3. b. (IV.2) How many years have you studied in school? _____ Item Score: _____

D. *Dependency (Females)*

Ideal Measure

1. a. (III.1) Ought to consult with another: Yes _____ No _____

Actual Measure

1. b. (IV.10) Did consult with another: Yes _____ No _____

How many? _____

Item Score: _____

Ideal Measure
    2. a. (IV.8) Respect from
          others
          Much _____ Little _____ Not Important _____

Actual Measure
    2. b. (III.8.9.10) Respect from
          Townpeople and
          neighbors: Much _____ Little _____
          One's own children: Much _____ Little _____
          One's husband: Much _____ Little _____
                                Item Score: _____

Ideal Measure
    3. a. (IV.9) Sensitivity to criti-
          cism of others:
          Serious _____ Light _____ Unimportant _____

Actual Measure
    3. b. (IV.7) Sensitivity to
          gossip: Yes _____ No _____
                                  Item Score: _____

E. *Personal Control of Affairs (Females)*
Ideal Measure
    1. a. (III.2) Working for
          another:
          Positive _____ Neutral _____ Negative _____

Actual Measure
    1. b. (IV.6) In last two years,
          have you worked for
          another?   Yes _____ No _____
                                  Item Score: _____

    2. a. (I.2) Sex of respondent:
          Male _____ Female _____
        b. (III.6) Life is more diffi-
          cult for:
          Males _____ Females _____ Equal _____
                                Item Score: _____

3. a. (I.3) Age of
respondent _____

   b. (III.7) Life is harder:
Before 40 _____ After 40 _____ Equal _____

Item Score: _____

Ideal Measure

4. a. (IV.5) A pair should live
in the house of:
Husband _____ Wife _____ No Difference _____

Actual Measure

4. b. (IV.1) The pair lives in
the house of:
Husband _____ Wife _____ Other _____

Item Score: _____

5. (III.21) Did the young couple (respondent) live with
the parental pair after
marriage?   Yes _____ No _____
If yes; less than 1 year ___

More than 1 year _____
How long _____

Item Score: _____

Ideal Measure

6. a. Ethnographic data: Children living at home are
expected *always* to help
their parents (For Chinantecs and Zapotecs.)

   b. (III.16) Do your children
help you?   Always _____
Sometimes _____
Never _____

Item Score:_____

GRAND TOTAL: _____

CLINICAL HISTORY

Number _____

Locality _____ Date _____
Name _____ Sex _____ Age _____
Occupation _____ Lives with spouse _____
Number of children living ___ Duration of complaint _____
Complaint _____
History _____

Pressure ____ /____ Pulse ×'_____ Breathing _____
I am going to read you a list of symptoms and would like you
to tell me whether they trouble you all the time, sometimes, or
never; are you troubled by headaches?

	Always	Sometimes	Never	Observations
1. Headaches?	_____	_____	____	_____
2. Noise in ears?	_____	_____	____	_____
3. Dizziness?	_____	_____	____	_____
4. Nausea on standing up?	_____	_____	____	_____
5. Difficulty in seeing?	_____	_____	____	_____
6. Does noise bother you?	_____	_____	____	_____
7. Do you feel cold?	_____	_____	____	_____
8. Migraine (headache and nausea)?	_____	_____	____	_____
9. Lack of appetite?	_____	_____	____	_____
10. Bad taste in mouth?	_____	_____	____	_____
11. Burning sensations in stomach?	_____	_____	____	_____
12. Stomach ache?	_____	_____	____	_____
13. Diarrhea?	_____	_____	____	_____
14. Blood in bowel movement?	_____	_____	____	_____
15. Constipation?	_____	_____	____	_____
16. Weakness; lacking strength to do your work?	_____	_____	____	_____
17. Are you tired after eating breakfast?	_____	_____	____	_____
18. Do you cough?	_____	_____	____	_____
19. Do you spit blood?	_____	_____	____	_____

20. Is it difficult for you to
    breathe?   ____ _____ ____ _____
21. Palpitations?   ____ _____ ____ _____
22. Do your feet swell?   ____ _____ ____ _____
23. Are your eyes swollen in
    the morning?   ____ _____ ____ _____
24. Do you lose consciousness?   ____ _____ ____ _____
25. Do you have pains in the
    chest?   ____ _____ ____ _____
26. Fever?   ____ _____ ____ _____
27. Do you have a burning
    sensation when you
    urinate?   ____ _____ ____ _____
28. Blood in urine?   ____ _____ ____ _____
29. Do you have aching
    throughout your body?   ____ _____ ____ _____
30. An ache in one part of
    your body? Which?   ____ _____ ____ _____
31. Do you have pimples?   ____ _____ ____ _____
32. Does your skin itch?   ____ _____ ____ _____
33. Do you suffer attacks?   ____ _____ ____ _____
34. Sleep badly?   ____ _____ ____ _____
35. Become very angry?   ____ _____ ____ _____
36. Have a desire to cry?   ____ _____ ____ _____
37. Do your hands sweat?   ____ _____ ____ _____
38. Are you unhappy when
    you work (in your fields;
    in housework)?   ____ _____ ____ _____
39. Suffer nightmares?   ____ _____ ____ _____
40. Sigh a lot?   ____ _____ ____ _____
41. How many times have nodules been removed? _____
42. Do you have any now? _____
43. Between the New Year and today, have you lost weight
    (a lot, a little, or none)? _____

PHYSICAL EXAMINATION

Difference between Pressure ___ /___ Pulse ×'_____
Breathing ×'_____
Temperature _____ Presentation: Healthy _____

All right _____

Sick _____ Weight _____

Stature _____ Eyes _____ Ears _____ Nose _____ Mouth _____

Head (nodules) _____ Neck (thyroids, veins) _____ Skin ____

Thorax (respiration) _____ Heart (bruits, arrythmia) _____

Abdomen: Masses _____ Pain _____ Liver _____ Spleen _____

Extremities: Varicoses _____ Arthritis _____ Cyanosis _____

Reflexes: _____ Muscular atrophy _____ Dermatosis _____

Onicomicosis _____

Summary of pathology found (physical) _____

_____

Patient's attitude during interview and examination _____

_____

44. Which important sickness have you suffered previously?

_____

45. Which important sicknesses has your family suffered? ____

_____

46. How many older siblings do you/did you have? _____
younger than you? _____ 47. Of all your brothers
and sisters, how many are alive now? _____
 48. What did the others die of? _____

_____

49. In all, how many children have you had? _____
50. Of those children no longer living, of what did they die?

_____

Diagnostic impression _____

_____

_____

Indications: _____

Laboratory examinations. Routine: _____ /_____
                         additional: _____

Laboratory Examinations by

Name: _____

Laboratorio de Análisis Clínicos

MELCHOR OCAMPO 103   TELEFONO 42-23   OAXACA, OAX.

DR. FERNANDO GALINDO ENRIQUEZ.   **DR. MIGUEL ANGEL REYES G.**

Nombre: RICARDO Hernández
Fecha: 19 -II - 71
Sol: EST. : MINERVA GOMEZ

CITOLOGIA HEMATICA

HEMOGLOBINA	14.3	grms. %	96 %	(N: H: 15.5 M. 14.8 grms. %*)
ERITROCITOS p. mm.³	5.140.000			(N: H: 4.5-6, M. 4.2-5.4 mill.)
LEUCOCITOS "	6.600			(N: 5,000-10,000)
HEMATOCRITO	45		%	(N: H: 40-54, M: 35-48%)
VOL. GL. MED.	86	micras¹		(N: 82-92)
Hb. GL. MED.	27	micro-microgramos		(N: 27-32)
CONC. MED. Hh. GL.	31		%	(N: 32-37)
ERITROSEDIMENTACION	10	mm. TEC. WINTROBE CORREGIDA		(N: H. 0-8, M: 0-10)
PLAQUETAS p. mm.³				(N: 250,000-500,000)

FORMULA LEUCOCITARIA				FORMULA DE SCHILLING		
N: Adultos		N: Adultos				Normal
LINFOCITOS 8	20-30 %	528	1000-3000 p. mm.³	MIELOCITOS	0	0
MONOCITOS 0	2-6 "	0	100-600 "	METAMIELOCITOS	0	0-1 "
EOSINOFILOS 35	1-4 "	2310	50-400 "	STAB	4	3-5 "
BASOFILOS 0	0-1 "	0	0-100 "	SEGMENTADOS	53	51-67 "
NEUTROFILOS 57	60-70 "	3762	3000-7000 "	I. SCHILLING	0.07	0.02-0.1

* CIFRAS PROMEDIO: H = Hombres   M = Mujeres

Atentamente.

Instructions for Scoring Gravity and Severity

I Definitions

Severity: The extent to which the disease(s) impede the person from carrying out customary activities.

Gravity: The extent to which the disease(s) bring the person closer to death.

II Scoring

Overall Scoring: Both gravity and severity will be scored by points. For each, the maximum points that can be scored are 40. A person who scores 40 points on severity will be considered totally incapacitated and unable to perform any of

Laboratorio de Análisis Clínicos

MELCHOR OCAMPO 103   TELEFONO 42-23   OAXACA, OAX.
DR. FERNANDO GALINDO ENRIQUEZ.   DR. MIGUEL ANGEL REYES G.

Nombre: CATALINA LUNA CASTRO.
Fecha: OCTUBRE 1971.
Sol:

EXAMEN COPROPARASITOSCOPICO
(Unica Muestra)

SE HICIERON EXAMENES EN FRESCO Y DE CONCENTRACION DE FAUST EN

LA MUESTRA RECIBIDA, HABIENDO ENCONTRADO:

QUISTES DE E. HISTOLITICA. HUEVECILLOS DE ASCARIS LUMBRICOIDES.

HEMBRAS, ADULTOS Y HUEVECILLOS DE OXIUROS.

ATENTAMENTE.

his or her customary obligations; a score of 20 indicates the person able to carry out only one-half of the usual activities. In gravity, 40 points indicate that the patient's death is imminent; a score of 20 indicates a point halfway between apparent good health and the person's demise.

Scoring by Sections: Scores will be provided each of the four sections, A through D, respectively. These sectins are: History, Symptoms and Family History, Physical Examination, and Laboratory Examinations. Each one of the sections is composed of from three to seven subsections, each of which may be scored independently of the others. The maximum score that can be earned in each section is 10 points.

III Procedure

First read the patient's protocol in its entirety in order to be able to form a general impression of the state of health, as much in relation to severity as to gravity.

Scoring Section A, History

1. What is the nature of the patient's complaint, its duration, or history? With respect to severity, a score of 10 points would be indicative of complete prostration, whereas a total of 5 points would mean that the person is reduced to only half of customary activities. In terms of gravity, a score of 10 advises that the patient is moribund, and 5 points indicates that he is midway between apparent good health and death.

2. Tendency.

3. Strength required to meet the demands of work tasks. If the protocol contains this response, use it to complement—in either positive or negative terms—the scoring of severity. Use it, to a lesser extent, to complement the evaluation of gravity.

4. Review the scores resulting from subsections of Section A; make sure that they are correct and reasonable in context of only 10 points allowable for each of the subsections; then enter total sum of points for Section A, on the right side of the page.

Scoring Section B, Symptoms and Family History

1. Sum the number of symptoms reported: Count the symptoms that are recorded as Always, Sometimes, or Never and indicate these results on the lines allocated for this purpose.

2. Of those symptoms reported as "always" present, indicate which are of a "subjective" nature and which are "objective" in the proper spaces.

    "Objective" symptoms are those which are responses to questions 13, 14, 18, 19, 22, 23, 24, 28, 31, 33, 37, 41, 42, 43.

    "Subjective" symptoms include repsonses to questions 1 through 8, and 9, 10, 11, 12, 15, 16, 17, 20, 21, 25, 26, 27, 29, 30, 32, 34, 35, 36, 38, 39, 40.

3. Note those "objective" and "subjective" symptoms which

are present only "sometimes" or "never." Check your results.

4. Score by awarding 1 point to each symptom that is reported as "always" present, and 0.5 point to those only "sometimes" present. The resulting total of the "objective" symptoms is to be inserted in the subtotals of both Severity and Gravity. Contrariwise, the resulting total of the "subjective" symptoms is to be inserted *only* in the subtotal column of Severity. It follows that the total score of Severity will include all symptoms reported, whereas the total Gravity score will consist uniquely of "objective" symptoms.

5. Disease fatalities in siblings. (Questions 46 and 47, of the Clinical History.)

a. Count the number of siblings living, including the patient.

b. This material will not enter into the scoring of Severity. It will be taken into account in scoring Gravity if the patient's problem appears to reflect diseases characteristic of his or her family. If the latter is true, award 1 point if the proportion of siblings still living is 75% of those ever living; 2 points if the proportion of those living is only between 50% and 74%; 3 points if it is a proportion between 25% and 49% of those ever living; and 4 points if it is as low as 25%.

6. Disease fatalities in children.

a. Establish the proportion that children still living represents of children ever alive (information found on the fourth line of Clinical History, and in question 49 of the History).

b. Assign 0 points to Severity if all children remain alive. If the proportion is between 75% and 100%, score 1 point for Severity. Between 50% and 74%, score 2 points; between 25% and 49%, score 3 points, and, when the proportion of children living is less than 25%, assign a score of 4 points to Severity. This consideration will not affect the Gravity scoring.

7. Review your evaluations of Section B and place your total point scores in the appropriate space on the right.

Scoring Section C, Physical Examination

1. Presentation and attitude of the patient. The patient's presentation of self will weigh on both Severity and Gravity scores. Healthy appearance scores 0; moderately healthy appearance receives a score of 0.5, and sickly appearance, 1 point. However, the patient's attitude should be kept in mind, to be used later in formulation of the disease diagnoses.

2. Systolic blood pressure, second measurement. If it is abnormal but seems not to be related to the other symptoms or to the history, it will be scored as an "objective" symptom. Points will be assigned Severity on the basis of the discomfort it causes, but to Gravity only as a reflection of the extent to which it endangers life.

3. Systolic blood pressure, difference between second and first readings. Assigned to Severity to reflect the discomfort related to a change in levels; to Gravity solely to indicate the extent to which the change imperils life.

4. Diastolic blood pressure, second measurement. Assign points to Severity according to the symptoms and incapacity for which it appears responsible; to Gravity to reflect its threat to the patient's life.

5. Diastolic blood pressure, difference between second and first readings. Assign points to Severity to indicate symptoms and incapacitating effects; Gravity points will reflect your judgment as to the extent to which it endangers the patient's life.

6. Pulse, second reading. Your point score should reflect the extent to which you consider the pulse rate to be abnormal (as an objective symptom), and what it appears to signify in interaction with other symptoms. Points assigned Gravity will reflect your clinical judgment as to the extent to which abnormality of pulse rate signifies a threat to the patient's life.

7. Pulse, differences in rates on second and first reading. Points assigned Severity will reflect the extent to which this change is associated with other symptoms or has an incapacitating effect. Points should be assigned Gravity to indicate how this change reflects on the state of the cardiovascular and emotional systems, respectively.

8. Respiration. To be treated similarly to pulse rate.

9. Temperature. A temperature, taken by mouth, of 38°C will receive 1 point; 39°C will receive 2 points; 40°C will be awarded 3 points. These points will be recorded in the Severity column only, except when temperature is higher than 40°C, when it may be included in the Gravity column, depending on its relationship to the patient's general state of health.

10. Abnormal findings. Severity, according to the incapacitation it causes. Gravity, to reflect the extent to which a patient's life is endangered.

11. Review your findings and calculate the extent to which this physical examination suggests the patient to be incapacitated by the problems discovered. Your evaluation of the implication of discrepancies found between second and first measures (e.g., systolic blood pressure, diastolic blood pressure, pulse, and respiration) for disease processes or emotional dynamics, may tell you much more about the patient's state of health than *any* of the specific abnormalities diagnosed. The maximum you can assign this section is 10 points. In a similar way, estimate the extent to which this physcial examination suggests the patient's life to be threatened by the problems it reveals.

Scoring Section D, Laboratory Examinations

Each of the six issues that make up this section should be evaluated in terms of the overall clinical impression thus far achieved. Should you not conceive of a relationship between, for example, an abnormality reported by the laboratory and the clinical impression, assign scores to both Severity and Gravity anyway, although in this case you will probably assign lower points than if you had noted such a relationship. (Even though there is no relationship between a finding of *Amoeba histolytica* and *Ancylostoma duodenale,* presence of both in a patient should be scored double that awarded other parasites. The point score will be increased still more when these appear to be associated with your gestalt clinical impression.)

Make Note of the Retrospective Diagnoses

There are tentative diagnoses and they include both organic and psychoemotional problems. Include each of the diagnoses at which you have arrived, separating them into, respectively, organic and psychoemotional classifications. Be sure to include those observations which you feel will contribute to obtaining a relatively complete clinical understanding of each patient.

Arrive at a Total Score

1. *Severity.* In accord with the diagnoses development and the clinical impression arrived at, score for estimated incapacitation, based on maximum score of 40 points.
2. *Gravity.* In similar form, based on a maximum possible score of 40 points, estimate the extent to which the patient has suffered diminishment of health so as to be threatened by death.

Carry the section scores to the summary column and write the totals in the spaces provided.

Comparison between scores arrived at by adding the subtotals corresponding to each section, and those achieved by a sum of the total symptoms and diagnoses. If there are differences between these two subtotals, review again the scoring within the respective sections and select the clinical criteria that seem most appropriate. If such a correction proves necessary, make a note of how the adjustment was made and why. Place the definitive total point scores in the spaces indicated.

Include your name at the bottom of the second page to facilitate comparisons of criteria and judgments at a later date.

Measures of Severity and Gravity

Location _____ Age _____ Sex _____

Identification Number of Individual _____

	Subtotal of Severity Gravity		Total of Severity Gravity	

A. *History*

1. Complaint, its history
   and duration   _____ _____

2. Tendency   _____ _____

3. Effort required to ac-
   complish customary
   tasks   _____ _____ _____ _____

B. *Symptoms and Family History*

1. Symptoms

	Always	Sometimes	Never
Objective	_____	_____	_____
Subjective	_____	_____	_____
Total	_____	_____	_____

_____ _____

2. Fatal disease in
   siblings   _____ _____

3. Fatal disease in
   children   _____ _____ _____ _____

C. *Physical Examination*

1. Patient's attitude _____ _____

2. Pressure (systolic)
   a. Second measure   _____ _____
   b. Discrepancy
      between second
      and first   _____ _____

3. Pressure (diastolic)
   a. Second measure   _____ _____
   b. Discrepancy
      between second
      and first   _____ _____

4. Pulse
   a. Second measure   _____ _____
   b. Discrepancy
      between second
      and first   _____ _____
5. Breathing
   a. Second measure   _____ _____
   b. Discrepancy
      between second
      and first   _____ _____
6. Temperature   _____ _____
7. Abnormal findings   _____ _____ _____ _____
D. *Laboratory Examinations*
   Blood:
1. Hemoglobin   _____ _____
2. Hematocrit   _____ _____
3. Sedimentation   _____ _____
4. Leukocytes   _____ _____
5. Increase in number of
   leukocytes   _____ _____
6. Parasites in stool   _____ _____ _____ _____
   Summary
A. History   _____ _____
B. Symptoms and
   Family History   _____ _____
C. Physical Examination   _____ _____
D. Laboratory
   Examination   _____ _____ _____ _____
   Retrospective Diagnosis
   Organic _____

_____

_____

   Psychoemotional _____

_____

_____

Name: _____

References

Adams, R. N., and A. J. Rubel
    1967   Sickness and Social Relations. *In* M. Nash, ed. Social Anthropology. Vol. 6. *Handbook of Middle American Indians.* Austin: University of Texas Press. Pp. 333–357.

Aguirre Beltrán, G.
    1963   Medicina Y. Mágia (*Colección de Antropologia Social 1.*) Mexico: Instituto Nacional Indigenista.

Appley, M. H., and R. Trumbull, eds.
    1967   *Psychological Stress: Issues in Research.* New York: Appleton-Century-Crofts.

Bahr, D. M., et al.
    1974   *Piman Shamanism and Staying Sickness.* Tucson: University of Arizona Press.

Barlett, P., and S. Low
    1980   Nervios in Rural Costa Rica. *Medical Anthropology* 4, 4: 523–559.

Billig, O., J. Gillin, and W. Davidson
    1948   Aspects of Personality and Culture in a Guatemalan Community: Ethnological and Rorschach Approaches. *Journal of Personality* 16: 153–187, 326–368.

Blonde, L., and F. Riddick
    1976   Hypoglycemia: The "Undisease," *Southern Medical Journal* 69, 10: 1261–1265.

Bolton, R.
    1981   Susto, Hostility, and Hypoglycemia. *Ethnology* XX, 4: 261–276.

Brodman, K., A. J. Erdmann, Jr., and H. G. Wolff
  1956   *Cornell Medical Index: Questionnaire Manual* (Revised 1956). Ithaca, N.Y.: Cornell University Medical College.

Brown, G. W.
  1974   Meaning, Measurement, and Stress of Life Events. *In* B. S. and B. P. Dohrenwend, eds. *Stressful Life Events: Their Nature and Effects.* New York: John Wiley & Sons. Pp. 217–243.

Carrasco, P.
  1960   Pagan Rituals and Beliefs Among the Chontal Indians of Oaxaca. *Anthropological Records* 20: 87–117.

Cassel, J., R. Patrick, and D. Jenkins
  1960   Epidemiological Analysis of the Health Implications of Culture Change. *Annals of the New York Academy of Science* 84: 938–949.

Caudill, W.
  1958   Effects of Social and Cultural Systems in Reactions to Stress. (*Memorandum to the Committee on Preventive Medicine and Social Science Research*) Pamphlet 14. New York: Social Science Research Council.

Chance, N.
  1962   Conceptual and Methodological Problems in Cross-Cultural Health Research. *American Journal of Public Health* 52: 410–417.

Chiappe Costa, M.
  1979   Nosografia Curanderil. *In* C. A. Seguin, ed. *Psiquiatria Folklórica: Shamanes y Curanderos.* Lima: Ediciones Ermar. Pp. 76–91.

Clark, M.
  1959   *Health in the Mexican–American Culture.* Berkeley and Los Angeles: University of California Press.

Comaroff, J.
  1978   Medicine and Culture: Some Anthropological

Perspectives. *Social Science and Medicine* 12B: 247–254.

Corbett, J. G.
1974   The Context of Politics in a Mexican Community: A Study in Constraints on System Capacity. Ph.D. dissertation, Stanford University.

Crandell, D. L., and B. P. Dohrenwend
1967   Some Relations Among Psychiatric Symptoms, Organic Illness, and Social Class. *American Journal of Psychiatry* 123: 1527–1538.

Dennis, P.
1973   The Oaxacan Village President as Political Middleman. *Ethnology* 12, 4: 419–427.

1967*a*   Conflictos por Tierras en el Valle de Oaxaca, (*Colección Sep-Ini #45*) Serie de Antropologia Social. México: Instituto Nacional Indigenista.

1967*b*   The Uses of Inter-Village Feuding. *Anthropological Quarterly* 49: 174–184.

Dohrenwend, B. S., and B. P. Dohrenwend, eds.
1974   *Stressful Life Events: Their Nature and Effects.* New York: John Wiley & Sons.

Donabedian, A.
1966   Evaluating the Quality of Medical Care. *Milbank Memorial Fund Quarterly* 44: 166–206.

Dow, J.
1975   The Otomí of the Northern Sierra de Puebla, Mexico: An Ethnographic Outline. *Monograph Series 12.* East Lansing: Latin American Studies Center, Michigan State University.

Driver, H. E.
1974   Culture Groups and Language Groups in Native North America. *In* J. Jorgenson, ed. *Comparative Studies by Harold E. Driver and Essays in His Honor.* Pp. 228–236.

Edwards, M. H.
1966   The Relationship of the Arthritic Patient to the

Community. *In* A. M. Lilienfeld and A. J. Gifford, eds. *Chronic Diseases and Public Health*. Baltimore: Johns Hopkins University Press. Pp. 747–754.

Eggan, F.
1954   Social Anthropology and the Method of Cross-Cultural Controlled Comparison. *American Anthropologist* 56: 743–761.

Eisenberg, L.
1977   Disease and Illness: Distinctions between Professional and Popular Ideas of Sickness. *Culture, Medicine and Psychiatry* 1: 9–23.

Elder, R., and R. M. Acheson
1970   New Haven Survey of Joint Diseases XIV. Social Class and Behavior in Response to Symptoms of Osteoarthrosis. *Milbank Memorial Fund Quarterly* XLVIII, 4, Part I: 449–502.

Engel, G.
1979   The Biomedical Model: A Procrustean Bed? *Man and Medicine* 4, 4: 257–275.

Fabrega, H., Jr.
1970   On the Specificity of Folk Illnesses. *Southwestern Journal of Anthropology* 26: 305–314.
1974   Disease and Social Behavior. Cambridge: MIT Press.

Fabrega, H., Jr., and G. McBee
1970   Validity Features of a Mental Health Questionnaire. *Social Science and Medicine* 4: 669–673.

Fabrega, H., Jr., and D. Silver
1973   *Illness and Shamanistic Curing in Zinacantan*. Stanford: Stanford University Press.

Finkler, K.
1980   Non-Medical Treatments and Their Outcomes. *Culture, Medicine and Psychiatry* 4: 221–310.

Foster, G. M.
1951   Some Wider Implications of Soul-Loss Illness

Among the Sierra Popoluca. In *Homenaje A Don Alfonso Caso*. Mexico: Imprenta Nueva. Pp. 167–174.

1965   Cultural Responses to Expressions of Envy in Tzintzuntzan. *Southwestern Journal of Anthropology* 21: 24–35.

Frake, C.
1961   The Diagnosis of Disease Among the Subanun of Mindanao. *American Anthropologist* 63: 113–132.

Gaitz, C. M., and J. Scott
1972   Age and the Measurement of Mental Health. *Journal of Health and Social Behavior* 13: 55–67.

Gillin, J.
1945   Magical Fright. *Psychiatry* 11: 387–400.
1947   *Moche: A Peruvian Coastal Community*. Washington, D.C.: (Institute of Social Anthropology), Smithsonian Institution.

Gove, W. R., and J. F. Tudor
1973   Adult Sex Roles and Mental Illness. *American Journal of Sociology* 78: 812–835.

Hart, D. V.
1969   Bisayan Filipino and Malayan Humoral Pathologies: Folk Medicine and Ethnohistory in Southeast Asia. *Southeast Asia Data Paper 76*. Ithaca: Cornell University Press.

Holmes, T. H., and M. Masuda
1974   Life Change and Illness Susceptibility. *In* B. S. and B. P. Dohrenwend, eds. *Stressful Life Events*. Pp. 45–72.

Howard, A. and R. A. Scott
1965   A Proposed Framework for the Analysis of Stress in the Human Organism. *Behavioral Science* 10: 141–160.

Kennedy, J. G.
1973   Cultural Psychiatry. *In* J. J. Honigmann, ed.

Handbook of Social and Cultural Anthropology. Chicago: Rand McNally and Company. Pp. 1119–1198.

1978   *Tarahumara of the Sierra Madre.* Arlington Heights, Ill.: AHM Publishing Company.

Kiev, A.

1968   *Curanderismo.* New York: Free Press.

Klein, J.

1978   Susto: The Anthropological Study of Diseases of Adaptation. *Social Science and Medicine* 12: 23–28.

Kleinman, A.

1973   Medicine's Symbolic Reality. *Inquiry* 16: 206–213.

1979   Sickness as Cultural Semantics: Issues for an Anthropological Medicine and Psychiatry. *In* P. Ahmed and G. V. Coelho, eds. *Toward New Definitions of Health: Psychosocial Dimensions.* New York: Plenum.

1980   Major Conceptual and Research Issues for Cultural (Anthropological) Psychiatry. *Culture, Medicine and Psychiatry* 4, 1: 3–13.

Kleinman, A., and L. H. Sung

1979   Why Do Indigenous Practitioners Successfully Heal? (Papers from a workshop on 'The Healing Process') A. J. Rubel, special ed. *Social Science and Medicine* 13B, 1: 3–26.

Kluckhohn, C.

1953   Universal Categories of Culture. *In* A. L. Kroeber, ed. *Anthropology Today.* Chicago: University of Chicago Press. Pp. 507–523.

Koos, E. L.

1954   *The Health of Regionville.* New York: Columbia University Press.

Krejci, John P.

1974   Leadership and Change in Two Mexican Villages. Ph.D. dissertation, University of Notre Dame.

Krejci, J. and J.
  1981   Recent Social Change and the Folk Illness Susto.
          Presented at the Annual Meetings, Central States
          Anthropological Society, Cincinnati.

Langner, T. S.
  1962   A Twenty-Two Item Screening Score of Psy-
          chiatric Symptoms Indicating Impairment. *Jour-
          nal of Health and Human Behavior* 3: 269–276.
  1965   Psychophysiological Symptoms and the Status of
          Women in Two Mexican Communities. *In* J. M.
          Murphy and A. H. Leighton, eds. *Approaches to
          Cross-Cultural Psychiatry*. Ithaca: Cornell Univer-
          sity Press. Pp. 360–392.

Lawrence, J. S.
  1966   Epidemiology of Rheumatoid Arthritis. *In* A. M.
          Lilienfeld, and A. J. Gifford, eds. *Chronic Diseases
          and Public Health*. Baltimore: Johns Hopkins Press.
          Pp. 755–759.

Lazarus, R. S.
  1967   Cognitive and Personality Factors Underlying
          Threat and Coping. *In* M. H. Appley and R.
          Turnbull, eds. *Psychological Stress*. New York:
          Appleton-Century-Crofts. Pp. 151–181.

León, C.
  1963   'El Espanto': Sus Implicaciones Psiquiatricas. *Acta
          Psiquiatria y Psicologia de América Latina* 9: 207–
          215.

Levi, L., ed.
  1971   *Society, Stress and Disease*. London: Oxford Uni-
          versity Press.

Levine, S. and N. A. Scotch, eds.
  1970   *Social Stress*. Chicago: Aldine Publishing
          Company.

Levi-Strauss, C.
  1963   *Structural Anthropology*. New York: Basic Books.

LeVine, R. A.
1970   Research Design in Anthropological Field Work.
        In R. Naroll and R. Cohen eds. *A Handbook of
        Method in Cultural Anthropology.* New York: Co-
        lumbia University Press. Pp. 183–195.

Lewis, G.
1975   *Knowledge of Illness in a Sepik Society.* London:
        Athlone Press.

Logan, M. H.
1979   Variations Regarding Susto Causality Among the
        Cakchiquel of Guatemala. *Culture, Medicine and
        Psychiatry* 3: 153–166.

Macmillan, A. M.
1957   The Health Opinion Survey: Technique for Es-
        timating Prevalence of Psychoneurotic and Re-
        lated Types of Disorder in Communities.
        Psychological Reports (Monograph Supplement 7).

Manis, J. G., et al.
1963   Validating a Mental Health Scale. *American So-
        ciological Review* 28: 108–116.

Marcus, J., and K. V. Flannery
1978   Ethnoscience of the Sixteenth Century Valley Za-
        potec. *In* R. I. Ford, ed. *The Nature and Status of
        Ethnobotany.* (Anthropological Papers #67, Mu-
        seum of Anthropology.) Ann Arbor: Museum of
        Anthropology. Pp. 51–79.

Martinez, C., and H. W. Martin
1966   Folk Diseases Among Urban Mexican-Ameri-
        cans: Etiology, Symptoms, and Treatment. *Jour-
        nal of the American Medical Association* 196: 147–
        150.

Marwick, M.
1965   *Sorcery in Its Social Setting.* Manchester: Man-
        chester University Press.

Mason, J. W.
1975   A Historical View of the Stress Field. *Journal of
        Stress Research* June: 22–36.

McGrath, J. E.
    1970   A Conceptual Formulation for Research on Stress.
                In J. E. McGrath ed. *Social and Psychological Fac-tors in Stress.* New York: Holt, Rinehart & Win-ston, Inc. Pp. 10–21.

Mechanic, D.
    1962   *Students Under Stress.* Glencoe, Ill.: The Free Press.

Meile, R. L., and W. E. Gregg
    1973   Dimensionality of the Index of Psychophysiolog-ical Stress. *Social Science and Medicine* 7: 643–648.

Metzger, D., and G. Williams
    1963   Tenejapa Medicine I: The Curer. *Southwestern Journal of Anthropology* 19: 216–234.

Morsy, S.
    1978   Sex Roles, Power and Illness in an Egyptian Vil-lage. *American Ethnologist* 5, 1: 137–150.

Mull, J. D., and D. S. Mull
    1981   Residents' Awareness of Folk Medicine Beliefs of Their Mexican Patients. *Journal of Medical Ed-ucation* 56: 520–522.

Muller, D. J.
    1972   Discussion of 'Langner's Psychiatric Impairment Scale.' *American Journal of Psychiatry* 128: 601.

Nash, J.
    1967   Death as a Way of Life. *American Anthropologist* 69, 5: 455–470.

Nash, M.
    1960   Witchcraft as Social Process in a Tzeltal Com-munity. *América Indígena* 20: 121–126.

O'Nell, C. W.
    1969   Human Development in a Zapotec Community with Emphasis on Aggression Control and Its Study in Dreams. Ph.D. dissertation, University of Chicago.
    1970   (Response to Seijas) *Medical Anthropology News-letter* 2: 1–2.

1972   Severity of Fright and Severity of Symptoms in the Susto Syndrome. *International Mental Health Research Newsletter XIV* Summer, 2: 4–5.

1975   An Investigation of Reported 'Fright' as a Factor in the Etiology of Susto, 'Magical Fright.' *Ethos* 3: 41–63.

O'Nell, C. W., and A. J. Rubel

1980   The Development and Use of a Gauge to Measure Social Stress in Three Meso–American Communities. *Ethnology* 19: 111–127.

O'Nell, C. W., A. J. Rubel, and R. Collado-Ardón

1978   An Assessment of Relationships Between Social and Organic Measures of a Folk Illness: One Direction in Research in Medical Anthropology. Presented at Annual Meetings of the Central States Anthropological Society, Notre Dame, Ind.

O'Nell, C. W., and H. A. Selby

1968   Sex Differences in the Incidence of Susto in Two Zapotec Pueblos: An Analysis of the Relationship Between Sex Role Expectations and a Folk Illness. *Ethnology* 7: 95–105.

Pages Larraya, F.

1967   *La Esquizofrenia en Tierra Aymaras y Quechuas.* Buenos Aires: Ediciones Drusa.

Palma, N. H.

1973   Estudio Antropológico de la Medicina Popular de la Puna Argentina. Buenos Aires: Editorial Cabargon.

Palma, N. H., and G. Torres Vildoza

1974   Propuesta de Criterio Antropológico para una Sistematización de las Componentes 'Teóricas' de la Medicina Popular, a Propósito de la Enfermedad del Susto. *Relaciones de la Sociedad Argentina de Antropologia* VIII: 161–171.

Panum, P. E.

1970   *Observations Made During the Epidemic of Measles on the Faroe Islands in the Year 1846.* New York: Delta Omega Society.

Pelligrino, E. D.
1963   Medicine, History and the Idea of Man. In *Medicine and Society.* (Annals of the American Academy of Political and Social Science, vol. 346.) J. A. Clausen and R. Straus, vol. eds. Pp. 9–20.

Permutt, M. A., et al.
1976   Evaluation of Diagnostic Tests for Reactive Hypoglycemia. In *Current Views on Hypoglycemia and Glucagon.* Proceedings of the Serono Symposium, vol. 30. D. Andreani et al., eds. New York: Academic Press. Pp. 269–282.

Redfield, R.
1956   *Peasant Society and Culture.* Chicago: University of Chicago Press.

Roberts, R. E., et al.
1973   Social Factors and Responses to a Mental Health Questionnaire. Presented at the American Sociological Association Meetings, New York.

Rubel, A. J.
1960   Concepts of Disease in Mexican-American Culture. *American Anthropologist* 62, October: 795–814.
1964   The Epidemiology of a Folk Illness: Susto in Hispanic America. *Ethnology* 3: 268–283.
1966   *Across the Tracks: Mexican-Americans in a Texas City.* Austin and London: University of Texas Press.
1970   (Response to Seijas). *Medical Anthropology Newsletter* 2: 2–3.
1977   'Limited Good' and 'Social Comparison': Two Theories, One Problem. *Ethos* 5: 224–238.

Sal y Rosas, F.
1958   El Mito del Jani o Susto de la Medicina Indígena

del Peru. *Revista de La Sanidad de Policia* 18: 167–210.

Saunders L.
1954   *Cultural Differences and Medical Care*. New York: Russell Sage Foundation.

Schader, R. I., et al.
1971   Langner's Psychiatric Impairment Scale: A Short Screening Device. *American Journal of Psychiatry* 128: 596–601.

Scott, R., and A. Howard
1970   Models of Stress. *In* S. Levine and N. A. Scotch, eds. *Social Stress*. Chicago: Aldine Publishing Company. Pp. 259–278.

Seijas, H.
1972   El Susto Como Categoria Etiológica. *Científica Venezolana* 23, Supl. 3: 176–178.
1973   An Approach to the Study of the Medical Aspects of Culture. *Current Anthropology* 14: 544–545.

Seiler, L. H.
1973   The 22-Item Scale Used in Field Studies of Mental Illness. *Journal of Health and Social Behavior* 14: 252–264.

Selye, H.
1956   *The Stress of Life*. New York: McGraw-Hill Book Company, Inc.
1974   *Stress Without Distress*. Philadelphia and New York: J. B. Lippincott Company.
1975   Confusion and Controversy in the Stress Field. *Journal of Human Stress*. June: 37–44.

Simons, R.
1980   The Resolution of the Latah Paradox. *Journal of Nervous and Mental Disease* 168, 4: 195–206.

Snow, J.
1965   *Snow on Cholera*. New York: Hafner.

Swadesh, M.
1967   Lexicostatistic Classification. N. A. McQuown, vol. ed. *Handbook of Middle American Indians,*

vol. 5. Austin: University of Texas Press. Pp. 79–117.

Tousignant, M.
1979   Espanto: A Dialogue with the Gods. *Culture, Medicine and Psychiatry* 3: 347–361.

Turner, V.
1967   *The Forest of Symbols*. Ithaca: Cornell University Press.

Uzzell, D.
1974   Susto Revisited: Illness as Strategic Role. *American Ethnologist* 1: 369–378.

Vogt, E. Z.
1969   *Zinacantan*. Cambridge: The Belknap Press.

White, K.
1972   Health Care Arrangements in the United States: A.D. 1972. *Milbank Memorial Fund Quarterly*. Pp. 17–40.

Whiting, J. W. M.
1954   The Cross-Cultural Method. *In* G. Lindzey, ed. *Handbook of Social Psychology*. Reading, Mass.: Addison-Wesley. Pp. 523–531.

Wyler, A. R., et al.
1971   Magnitude of Life Events and Seriousness of Illness. *Psychosomatic Medicine* XXXIII, 2: 115–122.

Yap, P. M.
1974   *Comparative Psychiatry: A Theoretical Framework*. M. P. Lau and A. B. Stokes, eds. Toronto: University of Toronto Press.

Zavala, C., S. Alatorre, and R. Lisker
1980   Distancias Génicas Entre Algunos Grupos Indígenas Mexicanos. Presented at the Congreso Interno of the Instituto de Investigaciones Antropológicas, Universidad Nacional Autónoma de México.

Zborowski, M.
1952   Cultural Components in Response to Pain. *Journal of Social Issues* 8: 16–30.

Zola, I. K.
    1966   Culture and Symptoms: An Analysis of Patient's
                Presenting Complaints. *American Sociological Re-
                view* 31: 615–630.
IX Censo General de Población, 1970
    1971   Estado de Oaxaca, Vol. II, Datos por Municipio.
                México: Dirección General de Estadística.
Clasificación Internacional de Enfermedades
    1967   Eighth Revised Edition. Washington, D.C.: Or-
                ganización Panamericana de la Salud.

Author Index

Subject Index